THE ALGEBRA OF SUICIDE

by
Irving Berent, M.D.

*University of California
Los Angeles, California*

HUMAN SCIENCES PRESS, INC.

72 Fifth Avenue   3 Henrietta Street
NEW YORK, NY 10011 ● LONDON, WC2E 8LU

Printed in the United States of America
0 1 2 3 4 5 6 7 8 9   9 8 7 6 5 4 3 2 1

Library of Congress Cataloging in Publication Data

Berent, Irving.
    The algebra of suicide.

    Includes bibliographical references and index.
    1. Suicide. 2. Suicide—Prevention. I. Title.
HV6545.B42   362.2   81-4131
ISBN 0-89885-006-1   AACR2

CONTENTS

FOREWORD

Statistical data have contributed greatly to the public's marked awareness of the constant and tragic problem of suicide. A number of books and articles now reflect the seriousness of this issue using statistics for proper emphasis. Indeed, government funds have been obtained to finance mental health and suicide prevention centers—again influenced by the high regard statistics enjoys in the minds of many. For the most part, this respect has been richly earned. Utilizing the principle that events occurring close together in time may prove related to each other or closely interconnected, these statistics have been useful in yielding excellent clues regarding the etiologies of various problems.

However, in one sense the science of statistics has been too successful. For I believe that certain individuals, not usually statisticians, have led themselves to an erroneous assumption—namely, that God exists in the shape of a computer! The science of statistics has been elevated to the position of all-knowing God! All that is necessary is that we play with numbers and our computers long enough; all the answers to why suicide happens will then be forthcoming! Unfortunately, this just does not prove to be the case. We obtain numbers and numbers alone. The "why" remains a subjective phenomenon, an emotional phenomenon, and often, a mythical phenomenon. Hypotheses about the phenomenon of suicide can only be obtained from individuals. And individuals will constitute my source of data. Other psychiatrists and therapists have had experiences similar to mine, having gone through the emotional feelings of participating with suicide—potential or actual. And it is a difficult subject; one that most of us would rather not write about. For to do so involves a reliving of pain. To deal with emotion (and all agree that suicide is emotional), we will experience emotion. The fainthearted among us will once again welcome the objective blanket of statistics and disengage ourselves.

However, to the degree that we can stay with the subject, we may be able to get a handle on what will be lifesaving to certain individuals who come within our orbit. It is with this hope that I choose to relive some of my emotions and experiences with suicide victims.

The handle I refer to above is contained in a concept brought to my attention years ago by Viggo Jensen, M.D., and Thomas Petty, M.D. Basically, the premise is that the potential suicide wants to be rescued from his fate and emanates clues for this purpose. This idea is not in itself entirely new. But that there is an actual rescue fantasy—with designated rescuer(s)—is a more clearly stated formulation that may constructively sensitize our thinking and provide active lifesaving functions. Otherwise information about suicide tends to connote a passive hindsight view of the problem—one that leaves us academically interested but somewhat emotionally detached. Illustrative of this detachment would be the tendency to be bogged down with statistics and thereby miss our cues to be rescuers. The concept to rescue is not so strikingly new. But it needs reemphasis in this mire and sea of numbers in which potential rescuers may be stuck and ineffective.

Enlargement of this theme with various ramifications will thus constitute the main emphasis of this book. To keep the person alive is the first order of business. Subsequent therapy in most cases is understood; but again, my focus will be on the initial recognition of the problem. It is this initial recognition that is so crucial. Many of us have been elected rescuers without knowing it. Somehow we feel that suicidal persons would choose only those on high pedestals as their would-be rescuers—doctors, ministers, and so forth. Others among us—the doctors' receptionists and nurses, the ministers' secretaries, and the friends and relatives of the suicidal person—may find it difficult to realize that the potential victim is often turning to us for lifesaving. The idea is beyond our usual stereotypes. We don't realize the suicidal person can be so democratic!

Chapter 1

INTRODUCTION

As a cause of death, suicide ranks high—inordinately so among the young, for whom life would seem to hold so much. The cynicism of those who exaggerate the position that we have a right to suicide stems from the confusion and anger of those who have been unable to comprehend some rhyme or reason to such an action combined with the disappointment and frustration of those to whom a suicidal person has turned for help and guidance.

In general, people believe in magic (more or less) and have a tendency to project outward into the world everything good or bad that actually originates from themselves: up and outward—everything good is from God; down and outward—everything bad is from the devil. The result in exaggerated negative instances is the feeling of being victim of the fates. The original source of one's magical belief, of course, derives from our survival of the ministrations of the good (and bad) outside forces we much later call "Mom" and "Dad." Depending upon how far we have evolved from our earliest history, the old theme plays an inversely proportionate part in our current life wishes, hopes, desires for satisfaction, and ways we experience our lives when faced with disappointments.

ORIGINS OF MAGIC

If we let ourselves imagine the smallest of infants, the scenes allow us to recall instances where we have witnessed a baby during those days and weeks when he or she is first examining those wonderful objects: fingers, toes, genitals, what have you. As we observe, we realize the child reacts to these objects in seemingly the same manner as he may react to other wonderful objects: nipples of bottles or breasts; eyes, noses, and lips of mother, father, or whomever; and so on. The mishmash of impressions at this point of life allows no differentiation of self from the others. The skin, toes, fingers, genitals we much later integrate and call "me" have been infused with the sensations we much later call "mother, father, bottle, breast." This might be one way of saying our mother and father live inside us—are parts of us on some level acquired in some fashion as above. Where do they live in us? All over! In our skin, toes, tennis elbows, whatever. To the degree that our various parts function well, we are being served well by our parents. The physically ill, suicidal patient will later be discussed in these terms—namely, as not being served well.

Keeping the above pictures in mind, magic can be conceptualized as having its roots in the belief that the infant's basic needs are being satisfied "from out of the blue." When the baby is hungry or wet, things are stuffed into his mouth and his rear end is wiped and dried—all because he has cried or squirmed. What power! Just wishing has made it so! The gods have acted and all is well. The child has been rescued from its distress. This is magic in its good sense. To the degree the child's pleas are not immediately answered or too long delayed, the "powers" are bad. The devil is at work instead.

Similarly, when the "good" forces are predominantly operative, self-esteem is enhanced—the infant is getting good feedback. Not only are outside forces good, but the parts of the body (originally fused with these outside parts) that are later called "me" likewise are good: "I like me!" And of course, the reverse is also true. The extent and importance of this set of phenomena can be appreciated by recognizing the essential motif of *Snow White and the Seven Dwarfs:* "Mirror, mirror on the wall—Who is the fairest of them all?" Basically, this is a disguise. The evil queen or stepmother is really the bad little child pleading with her parent (the mirror) for good feedback: "Tell me you love me!" This represents a later stage of development but one dependent on the earliest infant stages. "I like me. I look good. You like me." These are the elementary universals or models.

HOAX? HEROICS? HALT!

HOAX? Through the years a differentiation of terms has evolved: Suicide versus suicide gesture. That such differentiation has been made suggests to me people's anger and indignation at being "fooled." We hate it! That our anger may stem from our having been extremely worried is simple to demonstrate. Worry is a horrible feeling to contain within us. Imagine a young mother on the beach during the summer, walking up and down, looking and inquiring about her lost toddler who she fears may have gone into the water and drowned. You see her becoming increasingly frantic as the minutes pass. Finally, she finds her baby safe. But what is her immediate reaction when she reaches the child? She gets angry! We have all seen this happen. What does it mean? The sensation of worry is so horrible (combined with sensations of guilt)—"Why did I let the child wander off?"—that the person who has evoked the sensation in us is literally hated for a few minutes. Only after she expresses the anger, can the mother pick the child up, kiss him, and comfort him.

How does this apply to the suicide person? For the moment we are talking about the "suicide-gesture" person. Ordinarily, this label is placed on the far larger group of people who attempt suicide and survive. The fact of their survival infers usually that someone in the environment has responded to the emergency or that the method utilized was not lethal. Our society tends to think that someone has just been calling "Wolf!". But when someone has been calling "Wolf" so many times that the responding individual, the "rescuer," is reaching the point of saying, "God damn it! Die already and leave me alone!," we have an extremely dangerous situation. The parents of a young man described their state of mind in just this fashion. They had been worked over with his depression, drug use, periods of psychosis, and demands. As rescuers of their son, they gradually had been reaching the point of complete emotional depletion. These parents had had their own difficulties and, in the various ways they adapted to their son's demands, inadvertently had contributed to the critical escalating spiral. It was not a surprise to hear them finally say to their son: "Better that you are dead so I can stop having to worry about you!" Admittedly, this represents an extreme situation. But my point is that *this* suicide-gesture person will succeed someday. His becoming an actual suicide statistic is (to use a statistical phrase) highly probable. To my mind there is no validity to the distinction between suicide gesture and suicide. It is often just a slim margin between life and death that separates the one from the other—and this margin from case to case is highly movable! There is no hoax!

HEROICS?. Often there seems to be a romantic aura of mystery and even grandeur about the suicide victim. He seems to court death—that which most of us fear. "At least I will master something in my life—my death!" is the message we seem to receive. At other times, the individual who has survived might be heard to say, "I couldn't even commit suicide right. I had to bungle it!!" The need to establish some control, even if it is to be one's suicide, takes on an omnipotent grandiose quality which can unfortunately be misinterpreted by would-be rescuers as "being on stage." As with "hoax" above, the world can too quickly feel it is being manipulated by the suicidal person. But, again, there are no heroics.

HALT! Certain individuals who would espouse a most liberal position could well take umbrage with this book. Their premise is that freedom should also include the freedom of taking one's own life, that psychiatrists and other therapists are meddling with the rights of their patients at best, while being totally ineffective at worst, and that such community endeavors as suicide prevention centers, hotlines, and concerned church groups have proven statistically ineffective and wastes of funds and time. Their comments have shock value and contribute to the stimulation of rejoinders, such as this response, that may help reformulate thought. Furthermore, I too am a believer in freedom. My definition may have certain modifications, but they are not to be construed as restrictions. My premise is that we (therapists and concerned individuals) have a right to intervene and give the potential victim a chance to reassess! My assumption is that if we are the recipients of messages connoting despair, we have not only the right to respond but also the moral responsibility to do so. Indeed, the suicidal person may well be hoping for it. When he is completely devoid of this hope, he will suicide, and then the question of our role as interfering agents in his freedom will be truly academic. We will not have gotten the message (or have been alerted to it). We are to believe in *halt*.

Chapter 2

THE WISH TO BE RESCUED

As mentioned earlier, certain authors[1] have emphasized a most practical point—namely, that the wish to be saved from a potential suicide exists and is conveyed to would-be rescuers by various clues ranging from the most subtle to the obvious. Also, depending upon the premorbid personality, the clues may be bizarre or "crazy" rather than clues of "normal" description. Likewise, the choice of rescuer or rescue fantasy may be diffuse or bizarre rather than clear or "normal." The assumption is that a form of communication is being delivered to a potential rescuer. Whether it is perceived and understood by the would-be rescuer is another issue. Of course, the age and sophistication of the would-be suicide person will also color the method and form of his communication.

BIZARRE TO NORMAL

As mentioned, bizarreness can be present not only in the action or mode of suicide itself but also in the rescue fantasy

[1]See, for example, "The FANTASY OF BEING RESCUED IN SUICIDE" by Jensen and Petty.

of the suicide victim. What may have the appearance of a relatively simple, straightforward act may have an elaborate fantasy behind it. Often we are only able to observe the act without having any comprehension of the underlying themes. To be able to evaluate these themes becomes crucial in further determining the persistence of suicide risk. A few examples of bizarre types follow.

A gambler who, after final financial losses, stuck an ice pick into his abdomen and lay down in his apartment at night fully expecting to die found himself alive the following morning and believed that Lady Luck was now on his side. He took himself to the emergency room of the general hospital, where he expected the surgeons would just remove the ice pick and let him go! However, it was not that simple. The surgeons operated in order to perform an exploratory examination to determine whether internal organs were damaged. Fortunately, or miraculously, the ice pick had produced no serious damage. But the surgeons, hearing and responding to the unusual tale, asked for psychiatric consultation. Following this, the patient was transferred to a protective service, where additional history was obtained. He was a single man in his fifties, who had been earning his livelihood as a printer. In the preceding several months, he had gone through savings of $10,000–15,000 in his gambling pursuits. The woman with whom he had been living had deserted him when the monies were no longer available. Indeed, Lady Luck had not proved kind to him. We almost laugh with incredulous disbelief at the veracity of this story. The originator of the following tale, however, knows the psychology of the desperate gambler.

A middle-aged executive had absconded with $100,000 of his company's funds, losing the total through his chronic gambling. Anticipating the accounting department's disclosure of his crime within the next 24 hours, he had determined to end his life by jumping from an exceedingly high bridge. Just as he was about to let go, an old gnarled hand clasped his tightly. "Don't do that," said the old toothless crone. "I can help you for a slight consideration!" After hearing his story, she continued, waving her hand in front of his face, "First, the $100,000 is now back in your company's vault. Second, you now have an additional $100,000 in your own private bank account. And third, you will have been promoted to vice president!'' With a sigh of relief, the gambler pulled himself back over the railing of the bridge and inquired, ''And the slight consideration?'' ''You must sleep with me tonight in a motel!'' declared the hag. A deal was a deal. The following morning as he was dressing, trying to leave as quickly as possible, the old girl turned over in bed and asked, ''Say, Sonnie, how old are you?'' ''Forty,'' he replied. ''Well,'' she said. ''Aren't you a little old to still believe in witches?''

Both gamblers, the one in reality and the one of the story, deceive themselves about the rescue value of Lady Luck, placing her in the position of an all-giving mother (or father)—the perpetual rescuer. As reality pokes holes in this delusion, the gambler succumbs to lower and lower depths of depression. The irony is further reflected and emphasized at the end of the second tale, when the protagonist, having been brought to the point of jumping from the bridge is still so willing to believe that luck, or magic as now embodied in the old hag will rescue him. The eagerness to accept the delusional appeal of magic distorts all the senses, including the visual! The actual patient mentioned above is likewise quick to trust Lady Luck again based on the fact that he was surprised to awake alive the morning after stabbing himself. That he could so repress or deny his true state of affairs represents the true area of his delusion—his life's balance was so precariously placed. Lady Luck as a rescuer is just not to be trusted. When the proposed rescuer is so nebulous or ethereal, the suicide person's chances for survival are slim indeed!

Another example of a bizarre type follows. An elevator operator, when questioned about the suicide victim that had jumped from the roof of a building, said, ''Strange. I remember that I was puzzled by why this man rode up and down the elevator so many times. I was just about to ask him why when he finally got off!'' In this instance, the fantasies of the victim were not known and, the proposed rescuer (the last one we know of) was unable to grasp the message. The bizarreness was more obvious in the act (riding up and down in the elevator) utilized to convey the victim's plea for help. Such unusual actions are signals to those in the immediate environment that all is not well with this person.

Bizarre types of psychotic degree can likewise be presented. For the most part, the rescuers are even more exaggerated than Lady Luck. The actions, too, will most likely be bizarre. Elaborate fantasies having a persecutory quality are frequently prominant. On the surface, the persecutors might seem to be the opposite of rescuers. For example, fleeing his would-be attackers making ready to impale him, the victim leaped from a 10-story building. From outward appearances to observers not knowing the operative fantasies in the victim's mind, a suicide had taken place. But was it? At first, we would be tempted to interpret the misfortune as strictly related to the man's panic. But is it so simple? Could it be that the persecuting outer forces represent part of the victim's mind, split off from and condemning the rest of him? Is it possible to consider the people to whom he yelled just prior to his jump as his hoped-for rescuers? We all have heard about the individual who calls the police and says, ''Stop me! I'm going to kill!'' Does not such a would-be murderer's victim represent part of himself (e.g., his symbolic mother, father, sibling)? So in our psychotic jumper, have we not then been witness to an individual (projected outward) killing himself (murdering himself, more accurately)?

I have deliberately run the risk of confusing the reader with these last questions and examples of bizarre types in order to make one point: such bizarre types, although they exist, represent a minute fraction of all suicides. A very minute fraction. The suicide person, by and large, is *not* to be regarded as crazy. He is comprehensible. Likewise, his rescue fantasy is, when obtained, understandable. If the reader were to persist in thinking of the suicide person as always being of the bizarre type, he will be inadvertently steered away from his vigilance for potential victims who, for a better name, will be called the "normal" types. The latter classification, I emphasize again, represents the largest group of suicides and will be the focus of my remaining discussions. Some examples of normal types follow.

An 18-year-old adolescent, having broken up with her boyfriend, descends the stairway in a long flowing gown with an emptied aspirin bottle in her hand. She walks toward her parents sitting in the living room. The rescuers (her parents) get her to the nearest hospital emergency room, where she is made to vomit or has her stomach pumped. Besides ministering to her physical needs her parents hopefully will be able to attend to her psyche as well—give her comfort and opportunity to vent her feelings about the boyfriend, reassure her of their love (a form of attention to her self-esteem), and in certain instances perhaps enlist further professional help.

Contrast the above with the following true story—similar and yet so different! An adolescent girl descends the stairs in a gown with an emptied bottle. She walks toward her mother and sisters. The mother starts for the door as if to leave the house! "Mother! Where are you going?" cries out one of the sisters. "I'm getting in the car and going to Aunt Susie's so that I can telephone for an ambulance." "But, Mother, Aunt Susie lives 15 miles away, and besides, *we* have a telephone!" The dialogue may not be absolutely accurate, but the gist of it was reported to me a number of years ago. How does one evaluate the rescuers in this family? What may underlie the mother's confusion? The sister seemed to know what should have been done. Why didn't the mother? Indeed, the mother appears to have wanted to give the aspirin in her daughter plenty of time to work! She reminds us of one of the earlier examples, where the parents wished their son dead as a means of putting a final end to their worries about him. This girl, too, had begun to wear her mother's patience thin by other emotional demands. The mother might also have had limitations or resentful feelings toward this daughter for neurotic reasons that initially were not the daughter's fault. (The topic of responsibility is reserved, however, for a later chapter of this book.) Even though we do not know which comes first, the chicken or the egg, we are still confronted with the mother as being a poor rescuer for this particular daughter at this particular time. Would we feel as comfortable allowing this girl to return home with her mother following stomach pumping as we would the preceding girl with her two parents? Would we be as apt to refrain from obtaining psychiatric consultation with this patient?

Unfortunately, either case might be construed by all too many people as "just little girls acting hysterically who need their fannies whipped." Such might be the reaction of judgmental groups, the majority being individuals much senior in age and experience, who think of themselves as being so certain about what "real" feelings exist in this world. The error in judgment is related to forgetting that what may be overwhelming to one individual may be only unpleasant to another or that with greater experience we are better armed to deal with traumas and not be as likely to be overwhelmed. But many of these adolescents, although young and seemingly inexperienced with the woes of life, die! Would the above case of the adolescent with the mother who gets confused go on in life to become an adult suicide? Does having a mother who has a tendency to be confused, for whatever reasons, contribute to poor self-esteem; to a reaching out for other mother-rescuers, who may have even less interest; and to eventual premature death? We often hear of the young girl or woman who may use her beautiful body to get some kind of adoration (rescue responses). But the transience of such a device becomes only too apparent, only too soon. Once again, we have to catch ourselves in the tendency to make value judgments that too often coincide with whether the suicide person lives or dies. If the person lives, he or she is to be condemned as being just a manipulator. Only death prevents or protects the victim from our rage at being fooled.

Another normal type could be illustrated by the middle-aged engineer laid off from work, who has never fired a weapon, telling his wife that he is going to buy a rifle and go hunting. He later shoots himself. Again, the victim may or may not die. But his choice of suicide method strikes more terror in us than does a bottle of aspirin, even though the latter can be equally lethal. However, it is just not likely that a 40-year-old man will descend a stairway with a bottle of aspirin. Such an action would be too transparent (to himself as well as to potential rescuers) and not compatible with the conception of his own depression. Pride still remains. And so, we must keep continually in mind that the age and experience of the suicidal person may determine the method utilized and the subtlety in which the rescue message is conveyed. Above all, a person in such a position does not want to be laughed at.

Granted, the whole question of being laughed at may well be submerged in the unconscious rather than being part of conscious deliberation. A conscious response to being laughed at was given by a young woman who was hospitalized following an overdose. One evening about 10 days after hospitalization she heard nurses and staff laughing at certain other patients. She quickly assumed that they could equally laugh at her and, once again, became horribly despondent. Finding a light bulb, she smashed it and was going to cut her throat when staff intervened. Subsequently, she described how she had begun to trust some of the staff, feeling that perhaps there could be ways of climbing out of her depression. But hearing their laughter was just confirmation that no one really cared; life was truly useless. The attempt is always serious.

To get back to the engineer. What are the ways his wife, the potential rescuer, might respond? The woman in all professed innocence could in retrospect say that she knew her husband was depressed but thought the new activity, hunting, might somehow bring him out of the ugly mood he had been in lately. Even more common would be a comment that the proposed rescuer felt awkward in confronting the suicidal person with his depression or thoughts for fear of stimulating something horrible. Myths still hang on. In contrast, the appropriate rescuer-wife would and should yell, scream if necessary at such a disclosure, thereby once more establishing emotional connection with her husband that could offer sustenance—either enough in itself or leading to additional help of a professional nature.

A third normal type could be the person suffering from cancer metastasis who seeks excess morphine from his nurse or doctor. Wherein such a situation can I see a rescuer? For all of us can empathize with this person and not be at all condemning. Indeed, to imagine that the person wants to be rescued, at first glance, seems really farfetched. But is it? He wants deliverance from his pain—overwhelming pain—primarily physical, yet also psychological. His body (fused condensations of mother, father and other important people in his life) has let him down. He is deserted and now at the real ending of his life wants bliss unending—the last sleep. There is no doubt that in his state of overwhelming crisis he wants deliverance. But is this deliverance to be suicide?

Those of us caring for such individuals frequently realize the patient does not want to be alone. His pain medications seem to have greater success when the patient is with someone loved. That the painful subject of death is actually talked about brings a form of relief to the sufferer as well as to the survivor. One wonders whether the subject of euthanasia is for some people a camouflaging "cover" for their inability to discuss openly with the dying one the emotions going on. Many current studies on the dying patient would suggest the longing of the dying person to have such a dialogue rather than shut off by pretense—"Oh! You'll be alright!" Having such a dialogue (and appropriate medication for pain) provides a rescuer. He does not have to die so alone.

In general, to the degree that we can identify with the potential suicide victim, we tend to call him normal, and some comprehension of the situation is available to us. The wish to be rescued does not contradict other wishes to die in the same person. This, too, leads to a camouflaging of the "clue" (suicide message) and confusion in the would-be rescuer. The balance of these two wishes can be precarious. Our emphasis has been on picking up on the wish to be rescued rather than discussing what and how treatment may be used to counter the wishes to self-destruct. We have to have a live patient to begin with!

"HELP STAMP OUT MENTAL HEALTH"

The old adage states that a picture is worth a thousand words. As a means of emphasizing how the suicide person wishes to be rescued, pictorial material obtained some years ago will be presented. The setting was a closed psychiatric unit of a military hospital early one morning. Upon entering the nursing station of the ward my eyes riveted upon a grotesque, although supposedly funny, poster that read Help Stamp Out Mental Health! (see Figure 2.1). Interested, I inquired of the nursing staff who the artist was and was told that several patients on the ward were "artists" but that the most likely individual was one who also that day happened to be sending out in the mail four extended cartoons.[2] When these cartoons were assembled by me in a particular sequence

[2]In general, the purpose of outgoing letter examination was to "protect" the patient. For example, discourage language or content that would disturb the reader or subsequently prove embarrassing to the writer. The writer would be informed of such screening and encouraged to make changes if appropriate.

(as numbered in Figure 2.2), the potential suicide implication was clearly seen.

Assigned to another psychiatrist, the patient now was being scheduled to return to duty after a hospitalization of several weeks. Upon first meeting, the patient presented himself as a seemingly well composed, partly condescending but not completely rude, cynical young man whose every gesture con-

veyed that he could care less about what was happening. He was going to be above it all as he acknowledged being the poster's artist. Within moments, however, this veneer dissolved when I announced to him that I also had read his cartoons in the outgoing mail and was terribly worried about him because I felt they must have been drawn in a particular sequence with the following meaning:

1. I'm hurting and being engulfed by my problems.
2. I must get myself to the hospital ("Call me an ambulance"), where I'll be helped.
3. Even though I'm at the hospital, no one is getting the message (observation deck).
4. Therefore, I've really had it. I'm dead!

The young man immediately broke down and cried. Sobbing, he went on to describe genuinely his predicament,

which had seemed to be a dead end. Through the years, he had alleviated his own tensions by drawing. From the ages of five or six, he would spend three to four hours a day in such activity. It was as necessary for his sense of well-being as smoking might be for someone else; without it, he would find himself increasingly restless and irritable. Fortunately, as a youngster, this behavior received approval from parents and teachers alike; he was a quiet boy, did not bother anyone.

When the time came for entering military service, he chose the branch he did because the recruiting official supposedly promised that he could draw and cartoon for the military magazine. But such did not prove to be the case. Instead, he was given routine enlistee work and orientation that from his point of view not only precluded his drawing be-

cause of lack of time but also considerably added to his tensions and anger with now no available discharge. He was rapidly becoming a time bomb. One could look at his hospitalization as a period in which he was to be defused. It was more his irritability that had been evident. Depression, as such, had not been obvious to those responsible for him. Ways by which other young men might alleviate their tensions and aggressions, such as swearing, griping, boozing, were not avenues apparently open for this artist. He was a good boy. One might reflect that often people of this age group who have made successful suicide attempts have been described as

good boys (or girls) and frequently as excellent students, quiet, not trouble makers.

But, at the time of making his drawings, the young patient knew that he had been scheduled to return to duty (to be discharged from the hospital). His period of hospital observation was now over. During hospitalization he has the time to draw (and partly defuse), and the personnel find him basically cooperative—a good boy. But as he realizes that he is not to be discharged from the service, as some of his hospitalized companions (diagnosed as having, for example, aggressive reaction or immature personality) are to be, his dilemma gradually dawns, as so vividly portrayed with his cartoons. One has to understand that a good boy cannot complain. It would be unmanly. He has to hope that by some magical means his message of despair will be picked up, and a discharge from service be extended him without his crying for one. That should be the doctor's decision and responsibility. He, the good boy, would just accept it.

I do not mean to imply that these thoughts were so clear (or conscious) to the young man. I am giving words to what has to be read between the lines of his behavior. Such a young man has a great deal of pride; this is also true for most potential suicidal persons, no matter what their age. It adds to the paradox of their needing help so desperately and yet camouflage their communications. In this regard, I should acknowledge that the reading of his cartoons had not been entirely accurate. The sequence in which I imagined the cartoons to have been drawn was essentially correct but in exactly reverse order (as I was later told by the artist, after he had composed himself and knew that I would work in his behalf). In other words, the artist drew from the most current feeling backward:

4. I've really had it. There is no way because...
3. ...no one is getting the message even though I'm in a hospital...
2. ...a hospital to which I engineered my own admission...
1. ...because I've been so hurting and engulfed by my problems.

I do not want the reader to assume that one has to be *perfect* to be a rescuer. We don't have to have a crystal ball. Instead, we should just go with our feelings. We'll be on target. We may not always have the clues posted on bulletin boards or sent through the mails, but something may grab our attention. The suicide person frequently has conjured up more than one rescuer, although one prime person may at times be elected. The above patient starts with his poster, "Help Stamp Out Mental Health." Is he not enlisting *all* the viewers of this caricature to his aid? "Please! Someone get the message!" Only years later did I recognize that the poster was not just a caricature of psychiatric services in general but an actual caricature of the psychiatrist to whom he had originally been assigned. His rage and depression had been condensed into a portrait that was crying out for attention from both the staff and fellow patients. Similarly, if we at the hospital did not get the message, his plea was being delivered through the mails in the form of four cartoons to other rescuers. Would they have responded? Fortunately, they did not have to be put to the test—at this time.

For those interested in what immediately happened to the above young man, a short postscript is in order. After discussing our meeting with his assigned psychiatrist, it was decided that the young man should be discharged from service. While awaiting several weeks for administrative details, it was said that he was successful in obtaining a position in a large industry that would utilize his artistic talents commercially—to our knowledge, a happy ending.

At this point, the cynics among us might ask or protest: "Hey! Wait a moment! Weren't you guys bamboozled by this young kid? Didn't he just manipulate you into giving him what he wanted! Suicide?—Hell! He just faked you out! Come on! Where is your data to support this kind of presentation? Where are your statistics?"

If one would grant what statisticians themselves have said—namely, that the human brain still surpasses the best computers in complexity and function—the following reply might suffice. The input or programming of the typical psychiatrist has included a number of cases that register and make their indentations—the memory bank. When the human mind-computer is now asked for delivery of material on suicide, those brain cells can deliver. Seriously, my data represent a number of suicide persons who might be considered on a spectrum from those who indeed ended their lives to those who made abortive steps. In other words, inferences are made from a continuum of cases that contradicts the attitude that every successful suicide truly desired this end or, conversely, that every unsuccessful suicide did not (and does not) really want to die and was just manipulating a hell of a lot. This continuum is illustrated by additional military examples that might be compared with the one above.

At the period of time discussed, it was still somewhat patriotic to serve one's country. Public opinion was such that our country and leaders were being held in high respect. We were not yet involved in an unpopular war, nor was the country reeling from such scandals as Watergate. Thus, the typical military enlistee felt it appropriate to fulfill his commitment. A young man had his pride. If pressed by service or his own psychological makeup to the point of being overwhelmed, he most likely would turn up first on the general medical sick list (general practitioners in civilian practice will acknowledge that 70–80% of their patients have psychological troubles behind their presenting physical complaints), hoping consciously or unconsciously that one or another of his physical problems would warrant discharge. By the time a patient from this continuum would cut his wrists, he ordinarily would have had an extensive medical file (indications of subtle precursors of the wish to be rescued). If the authorities did not see fit to respond to this message and, unfortunately, just returned him to duty after sewing up his wrists, a more serious attempt might follow, as in the next example.

A man, trying to hang himself, nearly strangled. He required a tracheotomy and may have had some transient brain damage, also. (The hanging had been just a little too long with some oxygen lack, but short enough to have a live patient whose story of increasing pressure was rather similar and parallel to the cartoonist patient above). He, too, had offered clues to possible rescuers. No one would be too likely to call this man a manipulator; he came too close to actually killing himself.

One might ask, "What are some of these pressures in the military (or elsewhere) that result in such desperation, depression, and suicide?" Although my emphasis has been on the wish to be rescued, a few words may be in order. With all due respect to the military, its purposes and environment are generally more restrictive than those of civilian life and consequently inadvertently contribute to a narrowing of possibilities and alternatives to certain individuals. For example, a navy man who had jumped into the ocean from his ship after cutting his wrists was brought to our facility. He had been aboard ship for about 18 months prior to this episode. In part, his conflict had come about because he was too smart. Of markedly superior intelligence, he had gradually been avoided by others, which left him increasingly bored and discouraged in his attempts to seek intellectual stimulation. He had no options for further social contact; that was well determined, since his companions were limited to those of similar job assignment. A form of sensory deprivation had become his lot. Fearful fantasies were developing from an initial: "Am I strange?" Enlarging on these reveries while simultaneously wishing for companions, he had become progressively desperate. His first communication was to cut his wrists. When his would-be rescuers could only jeer at him and proclaim, "He's really crazy, that egghead!", he made his jump from ship. If the rescuer does not get the first message, one has to become more and more emphatic—to the point sometimes of actually dying.

When first seen by me, this young reddish haired, freckled-faced sailor presented himself in a courteous, shy, yet strong fashion. It had been some days since the suicide attempt; he had others besides the old companions with whom he could converse. The immediate stress was ended. His term of service was just about over, and the hospital represented his last duty station. My point is that there was no ulterior motive in his suicide attempt to get out of service earlier—his discharge was already scheduled before his jump. The attempt had been genuine—no ifs or ands about it. Likewise, his note shortly after getting into civilian life could not be construed as "buttering me up," for neither I nor any other military personnel had power over him at that point. Briefly, his note told of how he was now enrolled in a university, looking forward to a continued life of intellectual stimulation.

My emphasis on the above normal types has been to stress and stress again that such a category represents by far the largest group of potential suicidal persons—a number of whom do *not* survive. The more bizarre and psychotic individuals who commit suicide are more apt to capture the attention of newspaper readers and therefore influence stereotyped thinking in which craziness is seen as an obvious and necessary characteristic to be found in *all* potential suicide victims. Unfortunately, this erroneous assumption contributes to would-be rescuers tuning out the messages emanating from the normal suicide group. They miss the boat.

Chapter 3

MORE ABOUT SUICIDE VERSUS SUICIDE GESTURE

From the preceding examples, one can see how the distinction between suicide and suicide gesture is a serious misconception when considered from a pragmatic point of view. Admittedly, some of the normal types (e.g., the adolescent going down the staircase with empty aspirin container) seem so transparent from our more experienced position that it is difficult for us not to label such actions as gestures. We are lulled into a false sense of security and then have the freedom of expressing our annoyance. Some of the examples of the military personnel can equally be misconstrued as manipulation with the resultant designation, gestures. One of the major difficulties contributing to our confusion is the failure to appreciate that seriousness of method is a value judgment, based in part on age, experience, and specific knowledge. At the risk of sounding redundant, the 40-year-old engineer is not apt to walk down a staircase with an empty aspirin bottle in hand. A 40-year-old woman might walk down a staircase carrying an empty Seconal or Miltown bottle, having "slushed" it down with some alcohol. But even such a woman might be subject to the criticism that she should know better—that her husband or teenage youngster would *obviously* save her and get her to the emergency room of the local hospital. Yet a woman did make such a first attempt and followed it by closing herself in a garage with the car motor on. She died of carbon monoxide poisoning. Those who, before being impressed, would desire a more statistical evaluation of just how many go this way will not ordinarily be able to find such data. You do not learn to appreciate the seriousness of the situation by looking at the numbers; you learn by having been there. And you do not have to have been there more than once or twice!

LARGELY ACADEMIC

To further illustrate this concept of seriousness as related to age or experience, I shall borrow from statistical data. It is a supposed fact that among all the professions, medicine contributes the largest proportionate share of suicide victims. And among these doctors, psychiatrists are highest on the list! I am sure that this does not surprise those who have always felt that psychiatrists were nuts anyway. But for those of you who might like to consider another explanation of the data, let me elaborate as follows: First, doctors in general are knowledgeable about medication—dosages and toxic levels. Something like aspirin or even a few sleeping pills are kid's play. (But again, such is not the knowledge of a teenager, who can be dead serious in her attempt even though she may survive). A doctor will employ more potent medicines of a lethal nature and dosage if drugs are to be the method. Anything less would be an affront to his own sensibilities let alone what he thinks others would feel. His choice of method has to become increasingly dangerous, even though his wish for death may not be any more intense than that of another individual who has utilized a less dangerous method. The margin separating death and life has been thus reduced by the meth-od he has used. But, again, this does not necessarily corres-pond to the intensity with which he wishes to die. Even though rescuers may respond, the amount of time for a res-cue may be terribly reduced by the choice of method, so that death might be apt to result even though another individual with equal intent might live because another method and or less potent drug had been used.

If we complicate the picture a little further, we can ima-gine the psychiatrist suicide. He basically knows the same facts of drugs as does his other doctor colleagues. He, too, has gone to medical school. In addition, he will most likely know the same psychological factors that I am presenting the reader. He knows about the wish to be rescued. How then does he communicate his wish without being in his own mind so terribly obvious? You can be assured it will be subtle. Thus, not only will the method tend to have more built-in po-tential for being lethal, but also the proposed rescuer may re-ceive only glimmers of messages, all of which contribute to the suicide being more successful.

From the rescuer's side, an additional point should be stressed. The suicide person who has been a physician has been living the role of rescuer (of sorts) throughout his whole professional life. Now when he requires a rescuer (perhaps a person who has been rescued by him in the past!), it confuses the minds of those about him. The tables have turned! Each has a new role, and the roles have been reversed. Can the pro-posed rescuer believe the role now placed on him or her? Or does it remain too foreign? Once again, I wish to emphasize not that psychiatrists or doctors are more depressive but rather that their modes of suicide tend to be more lethal and (probably more importantly) their means of communicating their wishes to be rescued lend themselves to a greater possi-bility of being overlooked until too late.

In practice, attempting to distinguish suicide from sui-cide gesture is largely academic. Pragmatically, the issue of whether one ends up dead or alive does not necessarily coincide with the intensity of the desire for life or death. Nor does the method of the suicide attempt necessarily disclose the real intent (life or death). The suicide gesture of today may be the completed suicide of tomorrow. This is not a cliche. All suicidal persons extend their wishes to be rescued. For the most part, I have presented individuals who lived. Even though I have stressed the concept of a continuum, there is the possibility that my emphasis has not fully impressed the reader, or that the reader might still be saying to himself, "This wish to be rescued is still only applicable to those who live. Those who really want to die would not communicate such a wish." A certain amount of skepticism is healthy. In order to once more illustrate the issue, I shall go into another case in detail. This time a man *not* saved—Mr. X.

INTRODUCTION TO THE TERMINAL JOURNAL OF MR. X

We all know that suicide notes may frequently be left by suicide victims. Some of these notes may be brief; others rather lengthy. It is unusual to have a journal—a collection of thoughts during the six days prior to the suicide. External circumstances proved to combine with tragic outcome.

Visualize a large city hospital that was serving the acute psychiatric needs of the community at a time in the year when staff substitutions had just occurred. The normal hustle and bustle was intensified ten-fold; skeleton staffs had been operating during the Fourth of July holiday and admissions for psychiatric services tend to increase on holidays. New staff members required the attention and direction of older staff members who still had their usual functions. Into this teeming environment comes an extremely depressed man who does not speak English (to any practical degree), looking for help—a rescuer.

I do not wish to convey that the environment itself was *the* source of the man's death. His own emotional problems had initiated his being brought to the hospital in the first place. However, the ability of the hospital environment to supply a rescuer was terribly compromised. On the other hand, the extensive attempts to reach out for a rescuer by this man are seen so clearly within this background setting. Such attempts are universal, and that is the whole point of presenting the following journal, translated from notes found in the man's possession after his suicide.

The Terminal Journal of Mr. X

The patient was seen in the Outpatient Department on 2 July and admitted himself to the hospital on 3 July. His journal begins on 4 July, one day after admission and six days before his death.

FRIDAY, 4 JULY, P.M.

> Doctor examined me and gave me so many different kinds of medicine. After I took the medicine I got a hot spell in my whole body. I called the doctor immediately and they gave me another kind of medicine and that hot feeling left me. That scared me terribly and *I thought I would lose my mind.* And that's for sure. This place is not to get cured but a place where you have to be crazy. Of course, you can't say a word because they handle you like a crazy person. My nerves are so worn out being here and worrying what will really happen to me. I almost can say it: compared to how I was, now I am really sick. I haven't got a book or anything, an old television only; just an instrument to tie you with and very well-fed nurses, who, if someone is acting up, are able to throw you on your bed and throw chains on you. And this "cure" does nothing but take a person to his grave. For my own self, this is the only thing that is waiting for me because my wife brings me here and after this place *the cemetery.* Of course, Mr. Y is the one who helped her in this and now, much sooner, death in this crazy house. God give me strength and help me not to suffer long. Now I am counting. I want to prove by this that I am not crazy. [Counted forward and backward from 1 to 20.]

On July 2nd Mr. Y was with me [this was his Outpatient Department visit]. I told him how I am getting on with my health. My complaint was this: I do not have any appetite and I can't sleep good. I wonder if he said the right things [via interpretation]. I did not know before whether he was talking with my wife and what they said together about me, but he encouraged me that I would go into the hospital and that they would cure me and that they would give me more medicine for my complaints.

On the 3rd, without my wife, I went into the hospital. That day she doesn't come in. I was shut by myself. From now on they keep me here like a crazy person. After one half day of questioning they put me in a big room among some crazy people. On Friday (4th) my wife comes to visit me. She took my money. She does not leave me even 20 cents for bus fare and I have not seen her since."

This now is four days before death. Part of this letter was written on 7 July. As a preface to this letter, it should be remarked that the translator mentioned that the daughter in the family is a teenager going to school and also working in a department store, wishing to save some money to go to college. Her father was against it. The father did not permit the mother to keep the money she earned either. This letter is directed to the wife.

SUNDAY, 6 JULY, P.M.

Always worried about my family. This last few months I do not have any appetite. I was exhausted. Mr. Y and you double-crossed me and talked me into a crazy house. I know I was nervous, but whatever I was, one thing sure, I was not crazy. And here in this place every moment, whatever I do they are just looking at me. They just laugh at me like I was crazy. You promised me I would have a doctor who could speak my language. I have not seen one yet. You, my wife, on Friday (July 4) came in just to get the money, and since then you are not interested. Not even a tear. *No opportunity to talk to anybody. Who is going to help me?* There isn't anyone. My wife, she is not interested about me, only the money. Friday she took every cent away from me. Now, too, Mr. Y is guilty because he is the one who made it possible to put me in a crazy house.

Since I got a terrific headache I am suffering terrible, but I am not crazy. Only my soul is sick. Instead of curing they locked me up as a crazy person. I worked hard twenty-two years for my family. I never drank up a penny. I was always trying to make a decent living for my family. Here in this country I did not drink, not even a cent. I was saving because I wanted to have a few dollars on hand so somehow we might get through these hard times that we have right now. But what benefit have we gained? She said I was hiding the money and she knew it's in a blue handbag where we kept it for the last few months. She said this because she counted money and until now they never told me how much my daughter's earnings are and I don't know where my wife is putting her seven dollars and fifty cents each week. Since the little girl has been working she pays $7.00 board but I was paying all the bills, gas, electric, telephone, etc. I did not spend a penny foolishly because I did not want my family to suffer shortage. I made a statement whatever I spent. You can find it all on the table.

MONDAY, 7 JULY

Now this is Monday. I have got a terrific headache. I was taking some liquid green medicine but I know that's why I got a headache. Makes me very dizzy but I can't sleep. Everywhere there's a lock. Now it reminds me of a jail behind the iron curtain. That's why I escaped and left the ground where I was born. There the Communists locked me up. Here my wife and Mr. Y put me in. Not in the jail but in the crazy house. But I guess in a few days I will be free. God will forgive me. In that night he will help me. The only way out from here is just death...My dear little son—I lived without a father I know what's waiting for him...I don't want him to have the same life I had.

This entry was written two days before his death. It is a letter to Mr. Z. There is a preliminary thanking of him for teaching the writer English. He then goes into the main body of the letter which follows.

TUESDAY, 8 JULY.

I am sorry the situation and everything else turned against me.
I know somebody made a big mistake and probably now they
are glad. They put me in the crazy house. Mr. Y is the most
guilty. He was right there when they asked me about my health
and he never explained to me what was happening. He should
have explained to me in my language what the doctor was
saying. But he did not.

TUESDAY, LATER IN THE DAY, TO HIS WIFE

I am not crazy. Today I was talking with the doctor and he was
asking me why I was hitting my teenage daughter. You know
perfectly well why. She was heartless and too cold towards me.
When you were in the hospital you know how much I suffered
to know you were ill. [The wife had in fact been ill sometime
before and had been admitted to the hospital with a mis-
carriage.] You told me I was laughing at you but I was not. I
was worried about you. In case I did anything against you, I
did that because you and the children wanted to be independent, and you were figuring everybody should take care of
their own money. You know that recently I have been hiding
the money, but not for spending it for my own use. I just
wanted to save it. Out of the $36.00 compensation I bought
food for six to live out of it. I paid electric, telephone and all
expenses. You, my daughter, my own child, and Mr. Y, you
worked hand in hand and you stuck me in the crazy house.
Mr. Y is the one who sent me here. He talked me into it. He
told me what to say. I was going to get some medicine at that
time and I did not know it was just an excuse to talk me into
going for help and then after I am here they are all going to say
I am crazy. You sent me to death. Six days now I am suffering.
You know I have been in the jail and you know that I went
through an awful lot. Yesterday you promised you were going
to get me out. Now it's 3 o'clock and you are still not here.
Now I am positively sure you wanted me to die or go crazy.
And if I get crazy you might tell everybody I was not. Did I
ever commit a big sin against you? You sure pick out the most
horrible things for me. This is a terrible death for me.

[Addressing remark to Mr. Y.] I am suffering because you two talked me into coming into this place [Returning to his wife] God shall forgive you and, if I won't be here anymore, live happily. That's why I brought you here to America. I can't stand it any longer because everybody will think I was crazy. The doctor told me I am not crazy *but I don't believe it for my own self anymore.* I hug and kiss O. Don't write my sister the way I died.

TUESDAY, AGAIN LATER IN THE DAY—TWO DAYS BEFORE HIS DEATH: APPARENTLY ADDRESSED "TO WHOM IT MAY CONCERN."

My poor sister. If she only knew what was happening to me. How many times she writes that I should take care of myself. Now look where I am...I am suffering terribly. I can tell no one. Nor show it to anyone. For then I would be considered crazy. I have to pull myself together. That will be the only way I can get out of here. And definitely I want to show my dear wife I am not crazy. Tonight I wanted to hang myself. But seems like they don't want you to do that here in this place, because then everybody would laugh, and they would say, "You see, he was crazy." Someone [this is a reference to his wife] can look at me so coldly even though I am suffering. I am here suffering. I am here six days and since then she came in twice. Friday (4th) she came for the money and yesterday, 7th, again to give me some more heartache. She came in the last minute at 4 o'clock. She knew that it was not a visiting time but she acted as if she wanted to help me. *My dear God give me strength. I wanted to live. Don't let me be crazy in this pitiful place.*

WEDNESDAY, 9 JULY (ONE DAY BEFORE DEATH)

Today is Wednesday. All the night I heard a certain crazy person hollering. I heard them! [The translator comments that the writing at this point is very disturbed and scarcely legible.] The suffering came from the ladies' ward. What a screaming. Yesterday my wife sent me a Priest here. She wants me to confess my sins before I hang myself. She already has buried me. My daughter, a teenager. She's helping for my funeral already.

My wife, she knows I am an irritable person and get angry easily but I give in easily. My daughter says I am like a maniac. Once I was going to beat her up, my son, too, then my daughter, and then she scratched my face and my wife helped her. She says I was going to *choke* the daughter. I never tried to hurt her hard. They never said why I did it. In the evening I took some medicine because I had hard heart-beats. In the morning 4 A.M. I was up. Yesterday I told the Priest I am all well and it is not true because I am very sick. I don't even take any medicine. I just tried to straighten myself because I wanted to prove to my enemies I was not crazy. [The translator commented that here the writing seems nothing but scribbling.] I feel I am getting weaker and weaker and my family is like Judas with Christ—only I don't feel the nail holes in my hands and feet. Right now my soul is strong and I can concentrate, but my body is weaker and weaker. For days I have not eaten anything. I am not able to eat, just drink. Any liquid. Now I am helping with the cleaning on the ward and this helps me to forget. They think the medicine is helping me but they are making a mistake because—cutting off human hands and feet—they are able to do that but curing a sick soul, no doctor can do. Most of the men who work here don't even know what the soul is. These people know about dollars. So far I met one good doctor and he is very good. He wears glasses, psychiatrist. Has a brush cut. He is a very good doctor and he writes all day long. Here is a great big swollen up fat person. Whether or not he is a doctor I don't know. He is smoking a pipe all day long and always talking with someone. He is smiling but my suffering is not less. Now another one is worrying. Seems like he is not normal. I am disturbed to look at him. He thinks he is very, very smart, that other one. He too is smoking a pipe, very heavy and comes and goes, counting his money. A great big pipe hangs down. Looks like a captain on the sea. I think he is playing cards. Another one is a very tired looking lady who is coming in every day with a different dress. She comes in, when I am going too close to her, shoves me away. I know why. She thinks I am crazy. She won't talk to me. I was asking her to call you but she wouldn't do it. I hope God punishes her like He should. She should be crazy and finish her life here. Over there is someone who is acting up. I got clothes on me, very old dirty underwear. Of course, I don't care anymore. My bed has rubber sheets on it. Throughout the night it gives me a little heat. I have got food that is not for my stomach and for that reason I had rather drink than eat. I am very nervous. *When will my wife come in?* I am quite sure she has a lot of work to do or she is talking to her daughter, but I think if she is going to run out of money she took, $23.85—you will make a big inventory looking for the money and in case you find it I won't see you, I don't know when. This afternoon Mr. Y was here. *I sure did tell him!* [Mr. Y. subsequently told the translator how the patient had presented him with the rope: Tomorrow I will be dead!] He is the one who took me in this hospital. Of course he did not want to admit it and he told me there is another hospital nearby and he may be able to put me there. But he will be surprised pretty soon. Now I wanted to see if my dear wife comes in tomorrow and if she is going to take me out as a crazy person. He just was inquiring what's on my mind. Whether I am going home and what I am going to do. I know—I only want to get out of here. Now that terrible feeling is past me which bothered me and terrified me days before. Yes, my soul somehow was winner over my body and somehow [untranslatable scribbling]. There is a half-crazy man behind me tied up with ropes on the floor. He is talking constantly. This is the place Mr. Y and my dear wife sent me to get cured. *My dear God give me strength and help me live with my family.* I know as you it is going to be hard. Of course, I might say now eight days I am suffering in this filthy place where the humans are getting more sicker than when they came in. I get one more night. I would like to sleep this night. I am taking sleeping pills but 4 o'clock I wake up. Day before yesterday I wanted to take more sleeping medicine from the green liquid but the nurse jumped at me and called me crazy. But you are the crazy ones I say to him with the same voice and after that they wanted to chain me then which would indicate I was for sure crazy.

THURSDAY, 10 JULY (DAY OF DEATH)

Today, the 10th, Thursday, is the day. This morning supposedly I will be free. [Mr. Y had told him he was to be released after his wife spoke with the doctor.] I had a horrible night. Last night the whole group got very little sleeping pill. All night long kept on talking. I could not stay in bed past 4 A.M. How many times I walked around the room I do not know. In between I snoozed a little. Now I am writing this letter on the bed. My dear God what a terrible sick person I turned out to be. One of the patients who was chained down sat up on his bed and cried and his cries were terrible. I can't stand this. Dear God give me strength, just until at least I am able to get out to the hall. *Just do something!* Now I am remembering on the first day I was delivered to the ward up here. I recognized someone. Seems like it was a little hole that I could look through. Terrible. I was petrified. A man was strapped down on the bed. He jumped up and went toward the window and was screaming, no, no, no. I am petrified, I am terribly scared. I know that is the thing waiting for me.

9:45 A.M. (ONLY A FEW HOURS BEFORE DEATH)

Seems like Mr. Y. double-crossed me. [The writing is very terrible now according to the translator.] The doctor and you come take me away—and everybody else comes but you. I know why. Because you want to destroy me. (Translator's note: You can tell he was very disturbed because some words are not translatable; they are not even his mother tongue.] You can take me now but I will be dead. But I am not crazy. But I don't want to suffer any longer. That's enough. My mind is clear. You know I am going to die. *I was standing by the window half an hour. I was waiting for you to come but you did not come.* Now I have finished with my life. God be with you. Goodbye. To whoever will be responsible after this: *I am pleading for the law to punish the sinners.* This is my last wish. Mr. X.

Comments on the Journal

Most important to observe is the back and forth movement in the expressions of the precarious balance: to live or to suicide. Numerous times we see even within the note of one day the fluctuations of hope and despair.

Also prominent is the theme regarding his fear of going crazy. Whatever his problems and their combinations, their total impact was overwhelming, leaving the patient in a state of terror and powerlessness. Lest his mind crack and he go crazy, he must suicide—a last sense of mastery! One might speculate on the universal applications of this idea—fear of losing one's mind as a possible etiological ingredient in suicide—one actively prevents its happening by killing oneself! One has the impression that Mr. X even senses the bizarreness of his own developing paranoid feelings—that is, a conspiracy against him: "You [his wife], my daughter, my own child, and Mr. Y, you worked hand in hand and you stuck me in the crazy house." And of course, the language barrier contributed to the frustration and a further sense of unreality.

Extremely poignant is the futile searching for rescuers: his wife, Mr. Y—even to the point of showing him the rope. (And yet how can we blame Mr. Y, who would seem to have rejected his role as rescuer because it was too horrible and emotional to consider; or displacement of responsibility—"The doctors will know what to do!" might have been the rationale.) Others to whom Mr. X appealed included the doctors, listing their characteristics in more detail the day before his suicide; the tired woman (social worker) with a different dress on every day, again emphasizing that supplies were not forthcoming; his sister in Europe; God; and finally returning to his wife at the end (standing by the window "but you don't come!") with clear-cut anger! It is ironic that he could hear certain disturbed patients holler (beginning of 9 July), but not one of his potential rescuers heard his inner turmoil! Or heard it well enough! The full capacity of his rage is indicated also on 9 July, when he describes his wife's accusation that he was going to choke the daughter. In his subsequent hanging (choking), one sees in a dramatic concrete fashion the meaning of the phrase "anger turned inward," and one experiences a rather chilling sensation of comprehension of this foreshadowing detail.

Again, one needs to travel in one's thoughts from the hustle-bustle hospital microcosm to the macrocosm of the world at large. Instead of the harrassed doctors, tired social worker, and so on, one need only imagine the large world of tired spouse, preoccupied employer, and the like, to remind oneself that would-be rescuers are still human beings involved in their own lives, needs, and worries, with little extra energies available for the rescuer role. Mr. X's experience is not unique. Others too have given their signals, have shown their pieces of rope indicating their basic wish to live and be rescued, and yet have suicided when the prospective rescuers did not quite get the message.

If Mr. X had been an artist, would it have surprised the reader if he too had created a poster reading "Help Stamp Out Mental Health"? Is there really so much that is different going on in the minds of these two people—the one who dies and the one who lives? Look at the poster once again. Doesn't it condense all the ingredients of which Mr. X speaks? As mentioned earlier, only many years later in retrospect was it possible for me to recognize just how much the poster included when I finally recognized the face. The intensity of the anger and rage was so devastating that it had partly blinded me—it was too much. Just as it was too much for Mr. Y, and he, blinded, did not see the rope. Again, it took many years before I could return to the poster more objectively and see its further contents. In spirit, the artistic lines contain condensations of thought and anguish that are identical or parallel to the written feelings of Mr. X. Fortunately, the military man posted his material. Mr. X kept his in his pocket. But even this difference is balanced by Mr. X's trying to verbally communicate his distress (although poorly) to his would-be rescuers. Then, too, he pictured quite graphically his rope to Mr. Y. So, we cannot assume that Mr. X's keeping his "pictures" in his pocket therefore makes his psychic state so different from the military man who displayed his. Mr. X displayed. But the "poster" Mr. X presented had not been quite vivid enough! Sometimes one has to be hit between the eyes—"Help Stamp Out Mental Health!"—before ominous signs register! Or register fully enough.

Everything in the mind of the overwhelmed person is in a state of flux. Somehow an erroneous impression must be corrected right from the start. The reader might assume that emphasis regarding the wish to be rescued infers that once the rescuer is alerted, all is then well. A one-time rescue is all that it takes. This is not true. Consider the facts that both men, the military cartoonist and Mr. X, had had rescuers, at least to the extent that enough notice by others had occurred to result in their respective hospitalizations in the first place. Granted, even if suicide itself had not yet been considered—or only vaguely conceptualized—they were seen to be in trouble. Initially, the suicide person may elicit a response from a potential rescuer that would suggest promise of rescue. However, the rescuer can not stop with just promises. The follow-through has to begin almost simultaneously in order to prevent a relapse into the old sensations of futility with no escape. Such fragility of the potential suicides' mental states might otherwise contribute to the ultimate irony of being partially rescued only to die on the thresholds of rescue when follow-up was not fast enough or complete enough. Unless the rescuer has obtained a complete picture from the suicide person of his rescue wishes and until some active changes (outer world or inner) have been expedited, the potential of suicide remains, with the potential rescuer easily converted to yet another rejector—the *last* rejector.

Keeping this general idea in mind is extraordinarily difficult even for the author, who professes to be experienced in these matters. Another short example may suffice. I was called one day at 7:30 A.M. by a person I had never met asking for a psychiatric appointment. The unusual time of day put my antennae on alert. To make just an office appointment would not have necessitated such an early morning call. Acting on this assumption, I hesitated to make just an office appointment and instead commented that the person must be terribly upset to be calling so early. In response, there was confirmation, including descriptions of feeling unreal, tearfulness, and desperation. When I suggested immediate hospitalization rather than just an appointment, there was some initial wavering but then agreement as the suicidal person turned over the phone to the spouse, who took the directions to the hospital. The caller was admitted two to three hours later.

So far, so good. A rescue had been initiated. However, later in the day, after office hours and about six to seven hours after the patient's admission, we talked face to face for the first time. The patient described the dilemma, but simultaneously strongly voiced the desire to be released from the hospital. "I have to accept my difficult situation: the hours here in the hospital have made it clear. I can handle myself now. You must release me!" Feeling that all was not quite right, I pushed for the patient's remaining in the hospital for at least another day so that we could speak further. Basically, I felt the set of circumstances leading to the desperate 7:30 A.M. phone call had not changed that much. However, I was being seduced by the patient's now seeming composure and adamant desire for discharge. I had compromised in my statement by saying "Stay at least for another day." I should have said, "Stay until we *both* know what's best to do!" and not given an artificial time limit.

The following day on coming to visit the patient, bags were packed and spouse was present ready to convey the patient home. Again, strongly insistent on discharge, stating the dilemma was something that could now be handled and agreeing to an outpatient visit in my office where we could pursue clarifications, the patient professed control in such a fashion that I yielded to the request for discharge. Part of a weekend intervened, and two and a half days later the patient was dead of an overdose of medications previously hoarded—just one day prior to the scheduled office appointment! The spouse subsequently described to me having pointed out my office building to the patient just the day before, the fairly good spirits of the patient, and other hopeful indications. Indeed, the night of the suicide, the spouse was aware that the patient had gone to bed earlier than usual and was asleep faster and deeper than usual but attributed this all to the patient's having been overtired from the emotional experiences of the preceding days. The following morning the patient could not be aroused. The rescue follow-through had not been enough. Postmortems are hellish. Colleagues could reassure me, "We win a few, lose a few!" But, when our *own* patient dies, or our *own* friend or relative, such reassurances do not help.

My disclosure at this point is once again calculated to emphasize the danger of being but a partial rescuer. Once the role is taken on, it must be pursued actively, even with the patient's seeming protests to the contrary. Reanalyze with me for a moment the events. An upset person, who has obtained my name from the family doctor, calls me at 7:30 A.M. to be the potential rescuer. With a short telephone communication, there is agreement to go to the hospital, where *voluntary* admission occurs. Within six to seven hours, there seems to be a change of heart, a desire to be discharged. Once again upon urging, the patient remains. The rescuer is still functioning in his role.

For the critics who regard hospitalization as a jailing process, this case is most illustrative. At every point, this patient knows the legal rights. With voluntary admission, the patient can determine discharges as well. After only six hours in the hospital, the patient could have left after speaking with me the first time, or left even before our meeting. My whole point is that a mixture of pride ("I don't really need hospitalization, I'm not really a crazy person,"), ambivalence and dependence (discussed in Chapter 5), and contradictory wishes of living versus dying may convey to observers an intent for discharge, whereas the strength of the proposed rescuer is really being put to the test. If the patient's strength already has been depleted to a position of almost being overwhelmed, it becomes more understandable that the strength and consistency of the rescuer must be tested—and retested. Similarly, how much the proposed rescuer values the patient is also being put to the test in proportion to the active efforts made by the rescuer. If the rescuer does not push strongly enough (or long enough) for hospitalization in this instance, he has not demonstrated enough concern, or that he thinks the problems are serious enough, or that the upset person is worth enough. In this spirit, the actual times a patient may require legal commitment to a hospital may represent total commitment of the rescuer to his role rather than a violation of the rights of the suicidal person.

Commitment to the role of rescuer is an *ideal*. I think I have made plain in the above example some of the factors that interfere—even where the rescuer is a professional. Those of you who have had your own failures are not alone in having been infallible. Numerous additional factors are influencing us in our role of rescuer. To continue to hospitalize a patient seemingly against his or her will affronts the sensibilities of all freedom-loving individuals, including psychiatrists. In a similar way, many would-be rescuers—friends and relatives—feel reluctant about their roles as rescuers, fearing that they are treading on the privacy of their loved one: "I feel something is not quite right, but how do I broach the subject? I don't want to hurt his feelings." And then, there is the pride of the suicidal person. As previously emphasized, it is often tremendous, resulting in a muting of the rescue message to such an extent that it is not perceived. The whole idea of suicide, by being so horrendous, supplies yet another factor influencing the failure to mobilize our rescue efforts. We may be too stunned by the horror, to the point we literally do not see. These are just a few factors influencing our failure to function as the ideal rescuer. We have to give ourselves solace and yet simultaneously strive for the ideal. All this is human—our frailties and our idealism.

Chapter 4

ACUTE ASPECTS OF THE SUICIDE ATTEMPT

OVERWHELMING CRISIS

One might conceptualize the suicide response as an adaptation to an overwhelming crisis. It is always desperate, a withdrawal from life mixed with pleas for rescue. The word *overwhelming* is crucial. As stressed before, for a particular patient, his or her age and experience as well as general development may contribute to an inability to withstand a certain crisis that would be handled successfully by another. That does not make the situation any less overwhelming for the first person—nor any less potentially dangerous as far as the possibility of suicide.

It is also the nature of the crisis state that *time* usually can be most helpful—time in which one might gather his wits, resolve his traumas, restore self-esteem, and survive. From this follows the rationale and value of even temporary intervention: to allow the person in crisis time to reconstitute or digest the events of the crisis (also perhaps to lean on the would-be rescuer and borrow from his strength) in order to evolve possible alternatives to suicide. It is known that crisis frequently tends to stir up all the old areas of self-doubt, self-criticism, and times of rejection, the full emotional impact of which hits with tremendous intensity as if the old events had occurred only moments ago and all at once! This body of emotions weighs on the current life situation (often bad enough), making it indeed appear insurmountable. To have the time to distinguish clearly feelings of today as distinct from those of yesterday may aid in a more realistic adaptation. Again, an example of time working constructively might help clarify:

The woman had driven to a motel and there ingested a quantity of pills. Her husband soon discovered the event, and appropriate action ensued. The immediate circumstances were related to her anger at her husband, whom she felt had purposely mishandled their business and caused its financial failure in order to deprive her of accustomed social activities, friends, and style of life. Her readiness to see this business failure as her husband's rejection of her was, in part, conditioned by memories of arguments between her own parents that included such statements as the following. Mother to father, "If you leave, take *her* [the patient] with you!" "Alright, then, I won't go!" responded the father. The implication for the patient was that the mother wanted to get rid of her and that the father only stayed not to be straddled with her and that the father only stayed not to be saddled with facts were exact. It was emotional gospel for the woman, and it certainly colored the views of her life thereafter. Another factor conditioning her response to the financial failure was the necessity of obtaining work to augment whatever her husband might provide. In reality, the patient was competent, skilled in relations with others in organizations, and educated. However, actual working conflicted with her old stereotyped feelings that working made her less feminine. This was not thinking based on rationalizing being lazy or the like. Her image of herself already threatened, the element of working seemed to be the last step in stripping her of her womanhood, thereby making her seemingly further thwarted and overwhelmed by their financial crisis. Fortunately, a short period of hospitalization, which was voluntarily accepted, proved helpful in providing the woman time to sort out which of her feelings were appropriate for today and which for yesterday. Economic difficulties continued, but alternate plans were devised that fulfilled certain reality requirements as well as contributed an influx of self-esteem.

OTHER CONTRIBUTING FACTORS

DRUGS.   Marihuana, LSD, alcohol, etc. A young college student with apprehensions regarding his sexuality (a very common concern of this age group) is at a party where he has taken LSD and is having a "bad trip"—namely, he is reacting to one of his friends having called him a "mommie's boy." Stimulated by his friend's remarks, his subsequent preoccupations and self-evaluations became progressively negative. His breakup with a girlfriend several months earlier was now being seen as proof that his friend's remarks were accurate—he must really be queer, maybe his friend was really propositioning him. The remarks caused disparagement, accentuated by distorted perceptions and fragmentations neurologically induced by the drug but having obvious psychological reverberations as well. The young man, who previously had been coping, now almost overdosed and was found 24 hours later, with a subsequent nip-and-tuck survival.

To get back to the old theme: who were his rescuers? Briefly, when home from school on his previous semester vacation, he had asked his father to let him see a psychiatrist in order to discuss some of his feelings regarding the breakup with the girlfriend and other areas touching upon his self-esteem. At that time, both the young man and his father (who had made the referral of his son) were told that it would be important to follow through with therapy, whether in the home city or that of the university. The young man was most desirous of doing so. There was, however, some reluctance on the part of the father, who felt the issues were passing and not too severe. One of the difficulties that followed was an inherent one in which the young person wishes to maintain some pride in relationship to his father (or mother or any other rescuer) and mutes the full extent of his depressed feelings. The father, for his part, found it hard to acknowledge completely the son's troubles, because this would have left him vulnerable to worry which he would have rather put out of his mind. Four weeks later the father's anguish was pathetic to behold—but fortunately, the son survived.

It should be clear that no drug in itself causes suicide or puts the idea into the mind of the user. However, once a person is depressed or dwelling on self-disparagement, drugs contribute to a setting in which fantasies may snowball and another victim may be overwhelmed.

OVERWORK.   Although overwork is frequently listed as a contributing factor in suicides, the issue often turns out to be a matter of poor self-esteem. An example of the junior executive who has been expected to perform X amount of work might clarify the point. Not fulfilling the task or only doing so with extended hours makes the individual wonder if another person might perform with better quality and swiftness. Rather than having a superior who might commend him on his accomplishments, he is in a position similar to the youngster who comes home with all As and one B and the father (or mother) says, "Why the B?" I have seen such people in later life who do not look at this kind of story with humor—not at all. Their ulcers, hypertension, depression, and other stress-related ailments come to them honestly.

Another example of overwork is the young woman who has been up with a sick child for several days and nights and at the same time has been attempting to fulfill her usual chores. Will it be the work itself that is the trigger? Not ordinarily. Not unless she is already troubled with defeated feelings of housework, cleaning, catering to her husband, and the like, which for her have precluded other more stimulating fare. Sensory deprivation can happen at home just as easily as it can aboard a ship—as was the case of the sailor mentioned earlier. Self-depreciation is then a natural to ensue. Overwork just helps establish the setting.

ILLNESSES.   Even when illnesses in themselves are of a nonfatal nature, they too can help set the scene for potentially serious consequences. A surgeon colleague who ordinarily presents himself as a vibrant, successful individual confided at a lunch meeting of physicians in the following manner: "Irv, for the first time I know what depression is!" He went on to explain how he had recently been hospitalized for a period of a week with a back problem. During this time, he found himself becoming more irritable at his having to depend on nurses, other doctors, his wife. For someone as active as he, this forced dependence and restriction of activity (let alone the fact that his body had let him down) had combined to mobilize the depressive process. "I wouldn't commit suicide, but I knew the feeling a little." When I suggested that he had learned a great deal about the hospitalized patient and perhaps should give a talk on the subject at one of our hospital meetings—"It might be more impressive coming from a surgeon speaker than a psychiatrist," I had said—he concurred with the first part of my comment but declined to give the talk because a surgeon should not openly acknowledge such emotions in public! "Look, Irv, it's bad enough my referring colleagues know I've got some back trouble. They don't have to know that I might get emotional to boot!" Just to keep our main theme in mind: have you wondered whether my colleague was perhaps putting me into the role of would-be rescuer? If you have, then my message is coming through. Such a possibility would have to cross my mind. Fortunately, the physician in question was on the upswing. However, I felt more comfortable phoning him several days later to ask whether his back had continued healing and whether he was feeling less depressed. But it doesn't take too much imagination to picture another kind of outcome for a person with a comparable set of circumstances plus less emotional strength.

AGING AND DIMINISHED VITALITY. Although the usual concept of aging and diminished vitality would have a chronic or slow connotation, one that allows us a "getting used to" by gradual increments, acute awarenesses may really be the rule. The old joke in which the difference between anxiety and panic is given—anxiety being the first time you realize you can't do it for the second time; panic being the second time you realize you can't do it for the first time—epitomizes the subject in sexual terms. We learn of our aging in sudden, acute episodes, whether like the back spasm of my colleague or a tennis elbow. As mentioned in the Introduction, we tend to feel betrayed by our body parts that have been fused in our earliest experiences with the parts of our parents who were to sustain us magically forever. Once again, should our sense of emotional well-being lie in a precarious position, our additional poor physical state might prove to be enough to tip the balance to an overwhelming-crisis position. In addition to the symbolic betrayal by our parents represented by our diminished vitality, the fear of betrayal of the important people in our current lives might well be the issue. Is my spouse being faithful for instance.

ACTUAL LOSS OF IMPORTANT OTHERS. Divorce and death obviously may contribute blows that may be experienced as overwhelming. It is not so rare, for example, to hear a recent widow berate her dead husband in almost the same terms that a woman might exclaim against the spouse departing in divorce: "Why did you do this to me? Why did you leave me?"

We are accustomed to being aware of depression in such central survivors as spouses or parents of children who have died. Other survivors in the family may be equally affected but remain somewhat unnoticed as compared to the central ones. Two examples follow.

A man committed suicide. His wife and daughters were immediately stunned and subsequently (and what appeared appropriately) depressed for some time. The wife and one daughter gradually recovered, resuming their former activities although saddened. The other daughter remained depressed—indeed, distraught. Withdrawal, weight loss, crying spells mixed with apathy characterized her for some months. Consequent to a suicide attempt in which she cut her wrists, she had psychiatric consultation. Admittedly, a number of factors were involved, but one of the crucial ones was her guilt regarding certain events that had occurred between her father and herself months and years before his death. Now that he no longer was alive, there was no way of making it up to him. She would have to join him in death.

Unification with the loved dead one is a theme frequently described by writers as a motivation of suicide. Strikingly, the fantasy of unification illustrates the actual denial of death. For to be with the departed loved one certainly implies a continued consciousness (life) that is not extinguished by the suicide. Indeed, one hugs, is held and loved once more. Certain religious individuals (the young girl just described was one) have assumed this state of affairs throughout their lives. And such a philosophy can be very comforting and perhaps enticing. Those of us who remain more skeptical need not argue the existence of heaven with such a patient. Instead, encouragement to be reconciled with the living can be emphasized. A living rescuer (mother, sister), who need not be critical of the young girl's failings with her father, could gradually be accepted by the patient once the contents and motivations of her fantasy of reunification with her father were elaborated. In this instance, the therapist acts as a bridge (a rescuer of sorts) between her fantasy rescuer, the dead father who forgives her in the mystical world beyond, and her real-life rescuers, her mother and sister. Admittedly, the patient required hospitalization to provide safe time and space to effect the transition to real-life rescuers. It might be observed that the added time also allowed her mother and sister to resolve better their own mourning and become more available to the patient.

Unification with the loved dead one should be looked at in yet another way. In contrast to the above example in which the loved one is recently deceased, some suicides and suicide attempts have taken place in those who lost a parent years ago. For certain people, the fantasy operating during their whole lives could be expressed as follows. If only the parent had lived, he (or she) would have been able to help me when in trouble, advised me, and nurtured me, and my whole life would have been paradise. Granted, the feeling is being expressed in hyperbole, but for a particular emphasis. At times of crisis, fantasies that may have existed in rather attenuated forms take on great magnification to the point of becoming wishes magically realized. Fantasy rescuers because they are dead can take on a quality of "reality" during such periods that seems to far outweigh the balance of rescuers life provides. And all this can go on in individuals who are not psychotic! It is the nature of crisis that any one of us, no matter what our age and sophistication, can find our thinking so riddled with fantasy—fantasy that could conceivably fuel the last actions of our lives—that it is imperative that others about us step in and serve as down-to-earth rescuers until we are better able to help ourselves.

A second example provides yet another slant on the loss of an important loved one. A young person died in a car accident. The parents and siblings were grief struck with their loss. After a period of time, it seemed to be the youngest sibling, who still lived at home, who remained so despondent and expressed her suffering through poor schoolwork performance, increased obesity, and irritability. Finally, the youngster obtained the family's interest and was referred to a therapist. Then this young person related the fantasies of suicide in which the parents' (and older siblings') attention would now be focused on the potential suicide victim. In death, the limelight could be shared with the one who had died in the car.

We are too easily lulled into a false sense of security by what may seem to be overly dramatic reactions of individuals. The examples given were presented to the reader with just that aura—only to emphasize once again that the youth of the individual may contribute to such a quality, and we should not laugh it off. The young person described immediately above managed subsequently to choose companions among whom more car accidents than could be attributed just to chance occurred. One of the friends had had 23 traffic tickets within a year and a half! It became imperative to make just such an interpretation to the patient. No longer was suicide to be performed directly or in fantasy; instead, the exact duplication of the sibling's death was being sought—and in reality.

SYMBOLIC LOSS OF IMPORTANT OTHERS.   As mentioned in the foreword, suicide is a particularly frequent occurrence in the young age group. One wonders if an underlying motif is the fact that the young person is growing up and out of the proverbial nest thereby leaving the important others, the parents. And we know by this time that the leaving is frequently experienced as if the parents have deserted the children—paradoxical reversal. The timing of these crises may well coincide within weeks of graduation (whether high school or college), when usual expectations include being on one's own. We have all heard about the teenager who threatens the parent: "Boy! Just wait until I'm 18! Then it's within the law and I'll go. I'll show you. It'll be a relief not to be told what to do. You can stay out of my life!" And when 18 comes around, the parents are wondering and saying: "When are you going to go already? I'll pack your bags!" It's not usually this youngster about whom we have to worry. Such a person usually is more than able to express himself or herself! Instead, it's the youngster who may have presented little trouble during adolescence, was too quick to mind, rarely voiced criticism. Little trouble may too often mean compliance and resignation to being just the child, although a good one. Indeed, the role may be so entrenched that another role, young adult, is just too new a concept. As long as the role definition of being a child remains stable (there are classes to go to), all is well. With the props pulled out, the anxiety proves incapacitating. Headlines read: "School president, all A student suicides!" The role both of child and of student often is one well played, and that is the part that strikes us as being so uncanny. "Of all the students, he seemed to be the most mature!" Having not practiced the new role of emancipated young adult (through confrontations with parents or teachers), such young people can be overwhelmed. One young person having graduated college went to another university for graduate studies, where conceivably another three or more years were available. After a week the parents were called and rescued their child, who subsequently told a therapist, "I'm schizophrenic!" This was to justify the return home to the parents. The crisis of being in one's own small apartment rather than in the protected dormitory environment at the previous university was symbolically already too adult and split from the parents from whom separation had literally occurred during the previous years by distance but not psychologically. Geographically, the graduate school was much closer. But psychologically, it was a different world. Something had to be done!

In retrospect, one sees how the relationships of parent and child intertwine: the child hesitates to grow up and out; the parent may need extraordinary closeness (perhaps because of a lessened relationship with the spouse). Neither can let go. In this instance, the child can further rationalize its position by saying that "it would be the death of mother if she didn't have me to be concerned about!" And that might just be true. Where such rationalization is not available, the child may have no other recourse but panic, and suicide may occur. At least in the first instance, we have an opportunity with a live patient who may still present as deadened and be resistant to therapy because to improve already has built into it the ultimate aim of leaving the nest. Such progress can be very slow even at best. Such a patient not only has to give up the parent(s) but must also give up the old identity of child. These symbolic losses, when experienced gradually, we then call maturity. It is with the particularly vulnerable people that our rescuer role must be available. It is in the nature of making a point that one often has to cite exaggerated examples. The danger of such a procedure is that one can be misinterpreted, and the reader may conclude that suicide occurs only in such severe pathological cases, not in plain ordinary people. This is not the case.

Another danger that concerns me as I relate examples of young people is that the reader may inadvertently have been given an impression that any suicide is committed by an immature, if not actually psychotic, person. In the possibility that I have given this erroneous impression, several additional remarks might help to correct the situation. The mood of crisis or near crisis that is extended over a period of time is wearing. It erodes otherwise substantial and mature characters, making a shambles of them. *Regression* is a term, part of our psychiatric jargon, that infers the reawakening of earlier stages of development, with their corresponding qualities—fantasies, magical thinking, and immaturities. At the time of suicide, all these old methods of dealing with life become more apparent to the observer. In other words, the end result of the erosion process, not the process itself, is seen. Therefore, it is easy to assume the suicide person has been this way all along. Such an assumption could, unfortunately, lead to two additional thoughts: (1) if the suicidal person is really so immature, perhaps he deserves his fate; and (2) strong people of character would *never* perform such an act! By this time, I would hope the reader would no longer be vulnerable to such misconceptions.

As I consider the material about overwhelming that I have presented, I recognize that not enough emphasis has been given to erosion of the spirit. Characteristically, this erosion may be slow and gradual but incessant, without enough letup to allow restoration of well-being. Physical and/or mental resources are gradually sapped. Layers of maturity that supply the fuel energies of our coping mechanisms and simultaneously insulate us from various noxious stimuli of whatever sort (i.e., illness, economic reversals) are dissolved during periods in which erosion of the spirit occurs. The erosion process may be accomplished by little events rather than a gigantic single significant happening. However, the little events accumulate, and, if not enough recuperative time is available for homeostasis, they can prove devastating. The following essay explores this idea in detail. It uses primarily medical events, since it was prepared originally for a general medical audience.

CHRONIC UNRELENTING STRESS SYNDROME—CUSS

Chronic unrelenting stress syndrome (CUSS) is a phrase I have chosen to describe exaggerated conditions of body and mind resulting from the onslaught of such frequent trauma that individuals have been reduced to a state in which they are incapable of functioning, feeling powerless to control their destiny and wondering when the next blow from the Fates will occur.

I am not speaking of the group of people who, upon being inflicted by a trauma, can cuss out the Fates. Instead, this is a panicked group having marked erosion of the spirit, with such regressive features as magical thinking, some paranoia, and an underlying conviction that "I am bad—otherwise all this would not be happening to me." That patients of this group might be on the verge of suicide may stimulate the first psychiatric consultation, although more classic anxiety–panic symptoms, such as insomnia, hyperventilation, dizziness, and phobias, are the usual reasons for referral.

The severity of any *one* trauma is not necessarily congruent with the psychic state or result. The loss of a loved one or a heart attack may not in itself cause the above syndrome. Indeed, even multiple losses or inflictions of illness that occur simultaneously but with an implied noxious-free recovery period may not cause it. For erosion of the spirit occurs with the continual drops of stress, much as conditions produced by chronic drops of water on stone prove more caustic than one sudden flood.

The story of Job is illustrative. He was not a case of CUSS so much as a wiping out of family and possessions in almost one fell swoop. As you may remember, the Devil challenged God to demonstrate a worthy man on earth who would remain so even under duress. That Job survived this testing might have related more to his *not* being whittled away piece by piece. Upon showing his faith in the Lord, even with a few doubts, he and his wife were presented with another ten offspring, flocks, and other rewards. However, imagine the story but with each of his children dying separately. By the time acute mourning for one was just about over, the death of the next would occur. And then the diseases, and then his wife's death, and then the losses of his flocks, and so on. In other words, a little time is left for anxiety to accumulate in between episodes, but not enough time to quite resolve the previous trauma. This is an exaggerated picture of CUSS.

Figure 4.1 provides a conceptual model for CUSS, following Freud, Selye, and others. If one were to conceive of the self, including such ingredients as consciousness and identity, as being surrounded by a protective coat, much as our physical being has its skin, certain analogies prove useful. Just as our skins serve crucial homeostatic functions and may be vulnerable to continued stress (i.e., cancer of the skin secondary to too much sun), the protective coats of our psyches may give way to repeated stresses, whether from such internal stimuli as superego (consciences) and id (instinctual drives, hormones, chemistries, enzymes) or from such external stimuli as infections, accidents, and losses of loved ones and businesses. These external stimuli, I'll designate as coming from the Fates.

Just as our skins may heal from the occasional trauma with no residual effect and once more be intact, our psychic skins similarly can reconstitute. But again, just as cancer of the skin is said to occur more often in old scar tissue, indicating higher potential for vulnerability of the latter, old wounds of the psyche that have been covered over represent weak points.

Yet, another parallel about protective mechanisms is in order: just as the skin will tend to turn red and nerve endings register discomfort with too much sun exposure, the "psychic skin" registers with anxiety (a signal, to paraphrase Freud) when homeostasis is threatened, and the individual, where possible, will remove himself from the noxious stimulus ("fight or flight"). Up to this point, anxiety as a signal can be seen as most helpful. In the CUSS group, the anxiety signal

Figure 4.1   Conceptual Model for CUSS,
(following Freud, Selye, and others)

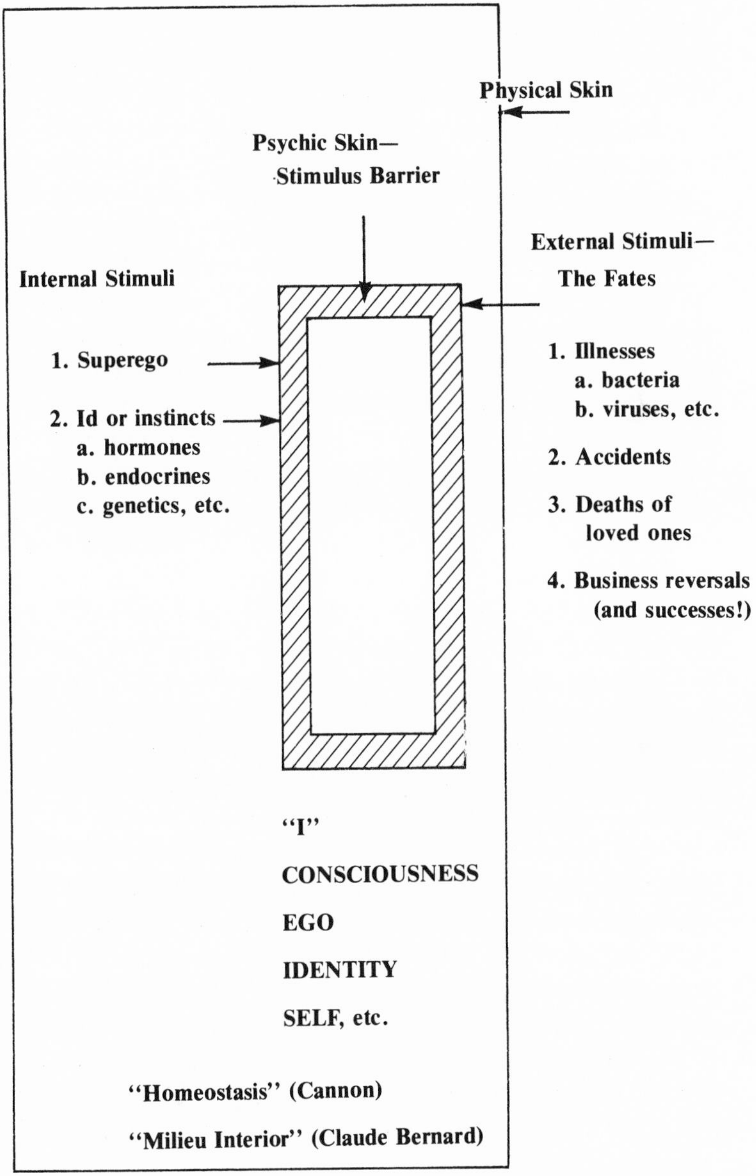

Physical Skin

Psychic Skin—
Stimulus Barrier

External Stimuli—
The Fates

Internal Stimuli

1. Superego

2. Id or instincts
   a. hormones
   b. endocrines
   c. genetics, etc.

1. Illnesses
   a. bacteria
   b. viruses, etc.

2. Accidents

3. Deaths of
   loved ones

4. Business reversals
   (and successes!)

"I"

CONSCIOUSNESS

EGO

IDENTITY

SELF, etc.

"Homeostasis" (Cannon)

"Milieu Interior" (Claude Bernard)

has gone haywire. Because of the too frequently experienced traumas, its alert system functions overtime and the least shadow on the wall is now experienced as a potential threat. In the process of being so experienced, each additional "shadow" has the power of disintegrating the "scab" the psychic skin has been so urgently attempting to produce. In the detailing of examples, this will be more clear.

Examples of CUSS

It was about 20 years ago while in the military service that I first became acutely aware of the phenomena being reported. The orthopedic service asked me to consult with a 20-year-old marine who had broken his wrist but nevertheless required hospitalization because he had developed bladder retention requiring indwelling catheterization and other in-hospital procedures. My orthopedic colleagues knew something psychological was happening but could not put their fingers on it. A broken wrist for a tough marine who had in earlier days survived the street gangs of Chicago did not seem to be enough stimulus to have so devastated their young patient. But upon reaching his ward and being given his chart, the answer lay in my hands. His chart was at least two to three inches thick! In his short year and a half of service, he had had a remarkable number of medical and surgical experiences, all of which were documented and legitimate. No one item (e.s., appendectomy, tonsillectomy, chicken pox) was by itself overwhelming. But as one considered the impact of the accumulation of these items over such a brief period of time, it was a little clearer why the broken wrist may have been the last straw.

A little more than two years ago, I was asked to consult at one of our local hospitals to give my impressions of a woman in her late thirties who had reported falling down some stairs and, while being worked up for possible head injury, developed bladder retention. This time I did not have a two-inch thick chart, although cataloging her medical experiences and those of her children in the preceding year would have yielded quite a thick one. She seemed to have a strange smile, however, which her physicians thought unusual. At any rate, I was in the position to see this woman frequently and continued to see her once she was released from the hospital. Approximately a year and a half prior to my seeing her, she had developed episodes of vaginal bleeding. Her father died several months later. She had a hysterectomy performed six months after that, with a preceding D&C complicated by urinary retention and bladder infections. And scattered throughout her own immediate group of medical and surgical difficulties were the tonsillitis, otitis media, injuries, and lacerations of her two active young children. Combined with this, she had her professional responsibilities as a registered nurse working with patients who were critically ill. It was many months after I began treatment with this woman that the mystery of her falling down stairs was cleared up. It represented a suicide equivalent. She had reached the point of having been so anxious about when the next trauma from the Fates would be delivered that she wanted to put an end to the horrible suspense and do away with herself.

A third patient, a 43-year-old businessman, was referred after extensive workups by many physicians for weakness, insomnia, chest pain, and dizziness. Approximately 13 years earlier, he had suffered a back injury at a building construction site that necessitated his being in a whole body cast for about a year. He subsequently made a good recovery ("had never been ill before") and remained well for a number of years, until several years ago when he experienced a spontaneous pneumothorax (collapsed lung) while hiking in the mountains with a friend. He recovered uneventfully but subsequently became more conscious of periods of weakness, dizziness, and some chest discomfort for which he sought, in

an increasingly panicked fashion, medical and surgical consultations. These consultations resulted in such procedures as
cardiac catheterizations, angiography of the carotids and
their branches, and thyroid workups, to the point that at the
time of referral at least $100,000 had been spent. (Granted,
the fact that 80% was covered by insurance the balance out of
pocket was still significant.) As the patient put it, ''I would
have consented to any procedure—even with calculated
chances of mortality—if only the magical answer could have
been found.'' As disappointment followed disappointment,
with anxiety increasing in an ever-spiraling fashion, he began
a series of malpractice suits against various physicians and
hospitals. He was going to have control over something!

A fourth patient, a young-looking man in his late
thirties, had been working as a roofer when episodes of dizziness had reached such proportions that he had to obtain a
medical leave of absence. Once again, general medical work-
up yielded no specific cause for his difficulty. After several
psychiatric consultations with him, the following history was
obtained. He had been in the Navy a number of years ago,
and his ship blew up. Some 40 men were killed, a number
injured, but the patient was ''alright.'' He remained active,
and ''things were okay'' until about three years prior to his
consultations with me. His mother had become depressed and
required hospitalization with shock therapy and eventually
made a good recovery. However, recently his father after
retirement had shown indications of having become depressed and was alluding to certain suicidal thoughts. In
between, the patient himself had had several accidents,
including broken fingers, an injured knee, and a dog bite on
the face that required plastic surgery. Currently, he was in the
process of attempting to get a business going that was at a
''make or break'' position. Attacks of hyperventilation
finally prompted psychiatric consultation.

Now, if I were to leave my description of these people in this matter-of-fact fashion, the most important ingredient would be missing—namely, the horror, the constant horror that characterizes the type of anxiety I am attempting to portray. Perhaps the readers might try with me to imagine themselves as the above patient, roughhousing on the carpet with his dog when the latter grabbed his face and bit into it. The patient, several years after the fact, could calmly relate the incident, how he must have accidentally hurt the animal during the wrestling. But the underlying horror of a face torn asunder gets combined with the other tragic happenings of the past and into the state of chronic anticipation of worse to come in the future.

A fifth example, a woman in her late fifties, developed symptoms such as hyperventilation several months after the recovery of her husband, who had had a myocardial infarction with cardiac arrest. Interestingly, she herself asked for psychiatric referral, recognizing that she had been reacting not only to the near death of her husband but also to the preceding actual death of her mother from a long, incapacitating cancer of the breast. Fortunately, arrangements were made where she could and would accompany her husband on his work as his assistant; family members who had been somewhat estranged became more attentive; and a sense of returning control rapidly followed. She was not reduced to a state where she had ceased to function as happened with this last example I will now report.

The case of Mr. L, a 25-year-old man, is extremely illustrative of the point that CUSS may be missed by every medical specialist—including the psychiatrist. About four years before Mr. L was seen by me, when he was a successful college senior, his car was struck by a truck, resulting in multiple injuries that included skull fracture, unconsciousness with a period of subsequent amnesia, and arm and leg fractures. In the next couple of years, there was gradual recovery to the point that he was able to play basketball and other sports. However, certain reconstructive work now was being suggested for his temporal mandibular joint, and a tumor (lipoma?) below his right eye was being considered for removal. A crescendo of anticipation and reawakened old feelings developed to the point that he attempted to overdose as his way of "finally ending it." According to the patient, the psychiatrist seeing him attempted to deal with his depression and "insisted" that he must have had a monstrous family background, been depressed for years, and should be in a psychiatric hospital until all these complexes were worked out. What the patient objected to and found most degrading was that he felt the focus never got onto his *anxiety*, which had been there in the first place. As he had to deal not only with the impending physical situations but now also with his being a "mental case to boot," it was no wonder that as time passed and insurances began to run out, my first consultation turned out to be in the setting of a chronic convalescent home—a place where he had been recently admitted in a state of being rolled up in a fetal position.

Comparison with Acute and Chronic Stress

After these various examples, I wish to emphasize once again that these people were by and large previously active, relatively successful (in their own ways) individuals. Table 4.1 summarizes several comparisons of CUSS with illnesses that might be categorized as acute or chronic. Of course, there are blendings, and the classifications should not be construed as absolute. There are a number of other differential considerations. Unfortunately, derogatory implications have existed as the various subtitles below indicate. One would hope that this form of prejudice would decrease in the future.

Table 4.1 Comparisons of CUSS with Acute and Chronic Stress

	Acute Stress	*CUSS*	*Chronic Stress*
Onset	Sudden	Often vague	Sudden, but later exacerbations
Time or duration	Fast with end-points	Semi-long but persistent	Long, often with well intervals
Number and type	Usually single, severe	Multiple. Into the syndrome— "piddling"[a]	Usually single but but may involve multiple systems
Symptoms	Specific	Vague, inconsistent, psychosomatic	Relatively specific (?) systems
Clarity of diagnosis	High	Vague	High
Number of physicians consulted	Few	Often many	Few
Feelings produced in physicians and in families	Empathy, challenge	Annoyance, suspiciousness, "What does the patient want?"	Empathic frustration
Iatrogenic dangers	Low	High	Low-moderate
Lawsuits	Low	High	Low-moderate
Erosion of the soul	Low	High	Moderate
Suicide risk	Low	High	Moderate

[a]piddling nature may account for the times a clinician is confused as to why a particular patient has sought his services (and may indefinitely continue!)

HYPOCHONDRIASIS.   Here there is a greater tendency to focus on various body parts with less overt anxiety. Obviously, the fine lines of separation blend. The general psychodynamic "If I can focus on a 'piddling' problem, nothing worse will happen" is probably common to both CUSS (far along in the process) and hypochondriasis. Indeed, perhaps the hypochondriac is a burned-out, more chronic CUSS variant. A detailed example is rather illuminating.

Mr. Z, a 60-year-old man, sought out psychiatric care for his apparent depression. He had had a heart attack five years previously but recovered and returned to work for several years, until he was "eased out" by unscrupulous partners about two years prior to my consulting with him. Since forced retirement, he had become more concerned with his bowel movements, to the point that he had devised a method of avoiding constipation by ingesting such large amounts of fluid that he had produced chemical imbalances that on several occasions were thought to have contributed to seizures. He also focused on other areas of his body: his heart (both parents had died of heart difficulties); some varicose veins that vascular surgeons felt were not necessary to operate upon (his sister had died following childbirth, supposedly secondary to effects of phlebothrombosis); prostate (his brother had cancer of the prostate). Yes, he was depressed. And the symbolic focus on some of these body parts kept "alive" some of the previously important people in his life. But now he also had marked anxiety and was wondering if he would live from day to day. Among other things, I confronted him with the fact that his underlying anxiety had turned him into a living death, that he was housebound, and that perhaps he should take a chance at life. He eventually sought out a hospice group, where the attitude of "live each day, day by day" appeared to give some comfort and support. Later, he began to work as a volunteer in a hospital setting (getting "protection" simultaneously), which at least allowed him to leave his house several times a week. Do we see this man as an example of CUSS, hypochondriasis, or depression? Perhaps all three.

MUNCHAUSEN SYNDROME.   As I have mentioned, some of the CUSS patients pursue their doctors with a vengeance, seeking any procedure that would seem to yield *the* answer to their problems and put an end to the anxiety that fuels their manifest symptoms, which to them portend doom. The much more rarely occurring Munchausen Syndrome (where people seek needless surgery and other medical treatment) I believe involves more overt masochism. Also, the patients give false identification, which indicates that their search for medical care is illegitimate in their own eyes. The psychic lives of these individuals have been miserable from day one. In some ways, they may represent the thoughts of an "abused child," who believes that love and affection come only after the beatings, illnesses, and other of life's hardships.

PSYCHOS (CONVERSION-HYSTERICS).   Ordinarily, physical illness (as documented by physicians) or accident plays a minor role in the history of "psychos." Yet even though triggered by other agents, anxiety, once present, may demonstrate itself with physical manifestations.

P.P.P. (PISS-POOR-PROTOPLASM).   This classification represents the "catchall" we have utilized to describe the "crocks," a further designation of condescension employed by certain physicians when confronted with their own inadequacies by patients difficult to treat. As previously mentioned and emphasized, the CUSS patients I have observed have previously functioned very well in their lives. That they may now be reduced to regressive positions, having once been sensitized by CUSS, is a result of the strength of unrelenting stress, not necessarily a reflection upon the original endowment of the patients.

GERIATRIC PATIENTS.   Our geriatric patients, just by having lived many years, are more likely to have experienced illnesses, important deaths in their families, and so on, to a point where CUSS is with them all the time. In this sense, senility might be a blessing. This group may well embody what the 35-year-old acute CUSS patient feels.

Traumatic Neurosis.   Freud referred to conditions in which revival of old memories, with their intensity of feeling, was precipitated by recent events. The anxiety and distress would now once more have to be mastered. The reader might recall the patient with the broken back who did not develop CUSS until many years later, after his spontaneous pneumothorax. Initially, he had described himself to me as having been in perfect health prior to his back injury. Only much later in treatment did history come out of his having had severe asthma for several years as a youngster. He had forgotten that. But one could speculate about the feeling tones reawakened at the time of his pneumothorax. In classical analytic theory, we often refer to these memories and groups of feelings as part of the childhood neurosis. Thus, if CUSS involves a current happening that is very closely tied to a very significant old trauma, one can see how a crescendo of anxiety may erupt without the series of numerous events ordinarily necessary to produce such a state of doom as illustrated in my other examples. And all these old feelings might well require a great deal of rehashing before a sense of mastery returns.

Treatment Considerations

Treatment is extraordinarily difficult for one very important reason. Once the stimulus barrier, or "psychic skin," has been broken, any additional stimulus, even if very small, is enough to keep the rupture open. For where can you place the patient into a completely protected cocoon? One would also have to protect the patient's whole family in a comparable fashion, because injuries to them also act as noxious stimuli upon the patient. Life goes on, and the Fates keep up their sporadic onslaught. For example, the lady who reported having fallen down the stairs was discovered to have a solitary thyroid nodule some months after beginning therapy with me when she had recovered enough to go for a routine back-to-work-physical. Being a "cold" nodule, a thyroidectomy was performed. Fortunately, it was not cancer, but the operation was still not an inconsequential procedure. When once again physically recovered (but now once more very much under the influence of CUSS), she could be equally shattered by such incidents as a neighbor calling and complaining about her little girl fighting with hers. Any event, major or minor could now be devastating. During this period of time, taking her son to the pediatrician for an ear infection could have her saying "If another thing happens, I don't know what I'll do" to the doctor who then would look perplexed at her and not know where she was coming from. Each new trauma reawakens the experiences of the preceding traumas—the impact of which hits as if the events had occurred just minutes before and all simultaneously.

The overall philosophy of treatment is to contribute to and/or reestablish a sense of control in the patient. To this end, the following steps are of value:

1. Have the patient write out a list of significant medical events that have occurred to himself and family. Any other traumatic events (divorces, business reversals) can also be listed. The process of doing so often is convincing to patients (and physicians) that their anxiety has come to them honestly. When the physician can make a statement to that effect and stress that physical manifestations of anxiety (e.g., hyperventilation, insomnia) are natural for individuals with the patient's experiences, he is making sense to the patient and also

countering the "I am bad" position which is a partial result of the patient's regression. Interestingly, on the surface these patients are often not in touch with their anxious thoughts but rather with their physical equivalents. One might ask, "Why is this anxiety masked?" The answer, I believe, is epitomized by a young boy who told me that he had some horrible nightmares but refused to describe them to me saying, "I may come to see you, but I'm not crazy! I'll get scared all over again if I tell you!" In a way, a similar mechanism is working within our CUSS patients to mask a great deal of the overt conscious anxiety. Similarly, people who lived through horrors such as the Holocaust and concentration camps do not ordinarily speak of their experiences.

2. Constant panic-anxiety does not bring out the best features of personality. It reduces a person, often in his or her own mind as well. Bladder and anal functions may often become disturbed as controls are eroded. This also contributes to the "I am bad" phenomenon. So, understanding how anxiety has accumulated tends to counter the above. "In knowledge there is strength." *Past* events lead to *present* anxiety (with physical concomitants) that convince patients of *future* calamity. To the degree we can demonstrate this, we have a workable lever with the patient as we interrupt this fallacy that has kept him or her in a state of panic.

3. Create a "protective umbrella" for the patient rather than too much dependency, which might subvert the awakening controls within the patient.

    a. Pay aggressive attention to details (especially non-invasive exams), and avoid iatrogenic effects. It is not infrequent that the patient mistakes a diagnostic procedure for a treatment. And this is interpreted as proof that there *is* something further wrong. And when the symptoms continue, the conclusion is that "I am going to die no matter what is done for me!" Thus, the clinician has to constantly keep in mind the psychological effects upon his patient produced by various procedures.

b.   Periodic appointments should be scheduled by the physician for monitoring purposes even when the patient has accepted a psychiatric referral. Not only is this helpful as far as acknowledging the possibility of human error (perhaps some condition was overlooked), but it also can be justified on the basis of attempting to "nip in the bud" any other physical consequences of chronic stress (e.g., ulcers, hypertension). Granted, this may cause the patient to take the position that the physician, too, is concerned about the Fates and thereby become more anxious. But explanation that emphasizes the reality of preventative medicine rather than the magic of doom usually is accepted as appropriate. In fact, the above actions may be used to counter some patients' self-deprecatory comments, such as "I guess it's all in my head." The physician's response could be: "You're right! It's *all* in your head! Yours and *mine*! Emotions, chemistries, and hormones *all* exist in our heads producing symptoms and problems. And that's why I'm going to continue to monitor you."

c.   Consider scheduling three-way meetings: patient, generalist, and psychiatrist. Often this may help cut through some of the distortions the patient may have. Three-way meetings that include patient, generalist, and patient's spouse may also be helpful in clarifying for the spouse how even "trivial" stimuli may exacerbate the difficulty. It may increase the spouse's tolerance and helpfulness.

4.   Although remaining aware of the fragile state of the patient, the physician should not undercut the patient's ef-

forts at self-help, nor should he be too solicitous. An internist friend demonstrated this beautifully at the end of a three-way meeting with our mutual patient: "Oh, Mr. S, could you please stop by the desk and speak to my aide regarding your outstanding bill! I'd appreciate your making some arrangements for more current payment!" When I first heard this, I was taken aback. But then I realized it conveyed to the patient that his doctor felt that he was not so fragile that realistic considerations were to be dropped. He, indeed, had strength and was expected to handle himself. How therapeutic!

5.   The use of medication may often be a problem. Whether drugs for insomnia at night or anxiety during the day are prescribed the implication is that the patient still does not have control over his life. My own response is to minimize the use of medications. However, as a compromise, small doses of diazepam (5 mg Valium) might be prescribed on a PRN (as necessary) basis: "You can take one every four hours only if you feel you must, but not more than four in any one day." The physician has prescribed the medication but has put some of the decision making (i.e., control) into the hands of his patient. Otherwise, the general problem is the tendency of the patient to attribute magic to the pill or doctor rather than to feel a sense of returning strength himself by being involved, at least in part in the decision to take medication and when.

Summary

1.   Admittedly, CUSS often represents a hindsight diagnosis. But where a patient presents a story of many workups, and physician consultations, the diagnosis should be considered.

2. CUSS conceptualizes a way of considering a number of patients seen in medical practice who have experienced (or are experiencing) severe anxiety with a sense of impending doom often disguised by physiological equivalents. Initially, many may deny anxiety even when asked.

3. Where we can demonstrate the legitimacy of the anxiety, we are offering the first steps to our patients' reconstitution with a sense of mastery and are countering their sense of being victims of Fate.

4. Other conditions might also be viewed as related to CUSS, providing us a mental set of greater empathy.

5. In our era of superspecialization, any one practitioner may not be as fully cognizant of all the medical stimuli going on in his patient, even when complete histories are obtained. Since he was not actually there and did not witness the many events, as his colleagues would have a generation or so ago, the current physician is apt to be left with "the facts and nothing but the facts" and be missing the horrible emotions that may have accumulated.

6. Body-mind relationships once again are epitomized by CUSS. The isolation of psychiatrists and analysts from their colleagues will, hopefully, continue to diminish.

7. The CUSS concept gives the clinician an emotional dimension to the word *overwhelmed*. It conveys a bit more of the horror our patients are experiencing. And it offers a rationale for appropriate medical intervention.

A CASE HISTORY

Recently, a patient (mentioned earlier in this chapter as an example of CUSS) supplied me with excerpts from her diary that illustrated in a remarkably striking fashion the above process of erosion, an erosion that went on relentlessly. Married with two small children, she additionally enjoyed working full time at her profession as a registered nurse in an intensive care unit with the critically ill. Life's responsibilities were great, but just prior to the beginning of these recorded events, she regarded herself as being quite happy with her lot. Similarly, the rest of the world would have regarded her as being both productive and content. According to the patient she began these medical diary entries as a means of better remembering and documenting the antibiotics given her son who had had various allergic reactions. The documentation, she felt, would be useful if and when other physicians' services were required, should she and her family be out of town or otherwise not near their own physician. Once she had become accustomed to jotting down the entries about him, she decided to include medical entries for herself and the rest of the family. The following material included the events of approximately one year prior to my originally consulting with her and continued for almost an additional year when, three weeks after deciding to leave therapy, she made a severe suicide attempt,which, fortunately, she survived. Upon once again resuming therapy, she spontaneously spoke of these notes for the first time and agreed to make me a copy that both of us could use to even better comprehend what had happened. Other than using different names for her children, spouse, and other people she mentions, the record remains essentially unedited and unabridged to better convey the subtleties of anguish that may accumulate with the CUSS process leading to a suicide decision.

To Dr. Irving Berent
The Months Preceding

Jan. 24th

Routine GYN check. Normal.

Jan. 27th

Sam has myringotomy (operative procedure) under local, in Dr. D's office for acute otitis media (ear infection). Rx. (treatment) Pro-penicillin I.M. B.i.d. X 10 days given by me at home. Sam was 2½ yrs. at this time and was very brave about his shots. I did not like to give him shots but he did suffer less than with his frequent episodes of vomiting and diarrhea with many oral antibiotics.

Jan. 30th

Possible flu symptoms.

Jan. 31st.

Heavy menstrual bleeding, thought of hemorrhage from I.U.D. Went to bed early at 8 p.m., to reduce bleeding and cramping.

Feb. 1st

Sat. 5 a.m. call from East. Dad had died that morning from broncho-pneumonia, an illness of 6 days. My sister was present as he looked at her then peacefully closed his eyes. Dad had been a heart invalid for 18 mths. I [sic.] died at home with his family, he had a fear of Hospitals.

I talked to my Mother and other family members, everything was under control and I felt that my mother had all the support that she needed.

My heavy bleeding had continued throughout the night. In the realization that I could not have traveled to the East before the Funeral, I told my Mother that I had Flu, rather than worry her about a possible hemorrhage, at this time.

The rest of the day was spent in bed, in the hopes that things would slow down.

I called my sister. She was very upset and had not thought about how ill he had been in the last 18 mths.

That day with the time that I had, I thought a lot about Dad and the fact that he was always happy.

I planned to call Dr. B on Monday regarding the bleeding.

Feb. 2nd

Sun. Hemorrhage abnormal, felt faint and weak. Called Dr. B at 1 P.M. Received telephone orders for Premarin X 15 days, the bleeding slowly subsided.

Feb. 3rd

My birthday, the first one without my Father. I did not know what to do about presents received. I felt ambivalent about having them. However, by then I was too weak to care.

Peter [husband] took me to see Dr. S. I had to lie on the couch being too weak to sit in the waiting room.

Feb. 4th

Report from Dr. S. Hemoglobin 9 gms. WBC's (white blood cells) 4.100. Diagnosis anemia and flu. Rx: vitron C with iron Q.D.

Dr. said that it would take about 2 mths before I was back to normal and he advised me not to push myself too much.

I thought about this and decided that 2 mths was too long to sit about and that I would just as well work. That was a full time 11-7 shift in cardiac care unit.

Feb. 7th

Sam to Dr. D, ear improving. Returned to work, after days off and 3 days personal leave.

Feb. 17th

Dolores [daughter], Dr. S. abcess incised, staph., Rx. Prostaphillin.

Feb. 24th

C.B.C. (complete blood count)

March 4th

Sam, Dr. S, abcess, Rx. Prostaphillin

March 13th

Bleeding, sudden with severe cramping that caused fainting, home from work at 4:30 A.M.

March 14th

Dr. B, attempt to remove I.U.D., unable to locate. Extremely painful procedure. X-ray at Hospital. I.U.D. out of position.

March 17th

C.B.C., Hb. 10, Hct. 33%, WBC 4.7. Returned to work.

March 18th

Bleeding with cramping, telephone call to Dr. B.

March 19th

D. & C. with removal of I.U.D. at Hos. Spent 1 hr. going from out-patient to in-patient admissions. The D. &. C. was scheduled for 12:30 P.M. Home at 4:30 P.M. Peter questioned this and talked to the Dr. Then the rounds of indecisions started.

The decision was to do it as an out-patient, then go home if ready. However when R.R. [Recovery Room] was due to close I was still asleep and was therefore admitted, for the night.

March 20th

Frequency during the night, abdominal (bladder) distension in A.M. Dr. ordered catheter, 1100cc residual urine. Discharged home on azo-gantrisan.

March 21st

2   Frequency, pain and abdominal distention. Called Dr. B was told that it was not his problem but that he would refer me to a urologist. 5:30 P.M. say Dr. P, cath'ed, residual 1000cc, home with Foley catheter.

March 25th

Dr. P, Foley discontinued.

April 2nd

9 A.M.Sam. Dr. S, acute otitis media, Rx. Ilosone. Returned to work C.C.U. (Critical Care Unit) 11-7 shift.

April 9th

Sam, Dr. S, ear improved.

April 11th

Unable to get satisfactory answers from Dr. B about the problems that I had experienced, decided that we had different views and so reluctantly sought another opinion.

April 14th

C.B.C., Hb 10 gms. Anemia followed by Dr. S.

May

Saw Dr. T and Dr. S at intervals, dates not recorded. Hysterrectomy was decided for treatment of heavy bleeding and anemia of 9-10 gms., with iron supplements.

May 28th

Flight to East, to visit my Mother.

June 3rd

Sam, many furunculi, visit to Dr., Rx. Amoxillan.

June 5th

Infection increasing, return to Dr. Garramycin started.

June 14th

In East also visiting with Peter's parents. Sam very sick with gastro-enteritis, fever and persistent skin infection. Local Dr. not easily available, planned to return home as soon as possible.

June 19th

Sam to Dr. Abbcess cultured, antibiotics held. I produced an abcess also. Rx. erythromycin. All cultures, staph.

June 21st

Sam. Return of severe diarrhea and vomiting. Visit to Dr. The 3rd different Dr. in this short visit. Rx. Lomital and Compazine.

Arrangements made for early return home.

June 24th

Sam very ill all night, flight booked for noon. Sam to Dr. for check before leaving. Some improvement after Compazine shot [followed].

June 25th

Sam—to Dr. S, Stool culture, neg. No new answers. Sam gradually improved on usual medications and diet.

July 8th

Dentist. Returned to work. Hb 10 gms. Inferon I.M. twice weekly x 2 wks.

July 11th

Hospital 3 P.M.

July 12th

Hysterectomy with appendectomy

July 15th

Hb. 9.6 Feosol; Feosol caused sever esophagitis.

July 19th

Am. I.V.'s, Foley Dc'd. Noon fainted when ambulating after Percodan. Eve. nausea and vomiting, abdomen distended, bladder pain. I.V.'s restarted. Foley reinserted.

July 23rd

Urine culture: staph. Keflin I.V.

July 27th

New Foley. I.V.'s and Keflin cont. until discharge; Dr. S office called but he was on vacation.

July 30th

Discharged with Foley. Dr. S to follow. No other problems.

Sept. 1st

A.M. called Dr. S because of increasing bladder pain and hematuria.

Sept. 2nd

Saw Dr.S, urologist.

Sept. 3rd

C/S (Culture and Sensitivity); E-coli. Rx. Ampicillin. Dolores, Dr. S, acute otitis media, Rx. Penicillin

Sept. 4th

Foley came out, talked to Dr. P and he agreed to let me try without.

Sept. 5th

Some distension and pain but do not want a Foley.

Sept. 6th

Sam to ER, chin sutured by Dr. W. Bladder problems persist.

Sept. 8th

Pain and distension unbearable, report to Dr. S, foley inserted in ER. High residual.

Sept. 10

Dr. T post-op check, everything OK apart from bladder. Dolores, Dr. S. ear OK.

Sept. 12

Abd. tender, hematuria, report to Dr. S, meds renewed.

Sept. 13th

Dolores, ear pain.

Sept. 14th

Dolores, Dr. S, acute otitis media. Antibiotic.

Sept. 17th

Dr. S, routine check re: nausea & vomiting in hospital, no tests, unless recurrence.

Sept. 19th

Dolores, Dr. D, ENT referred because of residual fluid in middle ear.

Sept. 22nd

Dolores & Sam, Dr. S for annual check, progressing well.

Sept. 24th

Dr. T, routine check, O.K.

Sept. 26th

Foley D'cd. A.M. Dr. S 3 P.M. 1000cc residual. Foley reinserted, Rx. Urecholine. 4 P.M. Dolores, Dr D, some fluid persists, for possible drainage. 5P.M. Sam, Dr. S, strept, throat, Rx. Keflex x 10 days. Shot in office.

Sept. 29th

Dolores, Dr. S, coughing. Wheezing picked up by me confirmed by Dr. Rx. Marex. Diagnosis made of mild asthma.

Sept. 30th

Sam, Dr. D, throat O.K.

Oct. 3rd

Dolores, Dr.S, injury to urinary meatus, thought to be caused by child's curiosity regarding Mother's Foley. Rx. Hot baths, observe for retention.

Oct. 6th

Foley D'cd., A.M. Dr. S 2 P.M. High residual. Foley reinserted. Dolores & Sam Dr. D. 4 P.M., both with different stages of acute otitis media.

Oct. 11th

Sam, cold.

Oct. 15th

CBC. BUN, ALB, FBS, Dr. S. Dolores DPT, Flu shot. Peter Flu shot. Sam not well enough.

Oct. 16th

Dolores, T. 103. Sam cough and fever 101-102 all week.

Oct. 17th

Sam has temperature 104.5, acute bronchitis & sinusistis, Rx. Erythromycin x 10 days. Changed to pediatrician closer to home with a group practice because of the children's continued problems.

Oct. 18th

Sam vomiting x 2, Donnatal Prn. Has been on Donnatal and lomital prn since age 6 mths for drug and food reactions or allergies.

Oct. 21st

Foley D'cd. A.M. Dr. S 2 P.M. Later at 5 P.M. increasing pain and distension; no baby sitter, had to wait for Peter to return, thought that I could manage, 9 P.M., ER. residual 1500 cc. T 102, Tylenol caused emesis. Foley again.

Oct. 23rd

Sam emesis, dehydrated, erythromycin held.

Oct. 28th.

Dolores, awake all night with ear pain, Dr. D. acute otitis media. Antibiotic.

Oct. 29th

Dr. S, HB 12 gms. Sam Dr. R. Bilateral acute otitis media, Bicillin.

Oct. 31st

Dr. S, 2 P.M. Cystoscopy was done in office on one visit date not recorded, bladder was said to be hypotonic, bladder wall was red.

Nov. 3rd

Dolores Dr. D, ear OK.

Nov. 5th

Dr. T, check. OK.

Nov. 6th

On ampicillin P.O. Onset of nausea and vomiting. Admitted to Hospital. Ampicillin I.V.

Nov. 7th

I.V.P. [Intravenous pyelogram]

Heard from East, Peter's Father had an acute MI [heart attack] but was doing well.

Nov. 10th

Dr. B; upper G.I., gall bladder, and blood tests.

Nov. 12th

Liver scan, blood cultures.

Nov. 14th

I.V.'s D'cd. Foley out. Residual 1750. Foley back.

Nov. 15th

Dr. K, GI consult O.K., beginning to feel guilty about all of these tests for perhaps just a drug reaction.

Nov. 16th

Calcium enzyme test.

Nov. 17th

Asked for Drixoral for sinus headache, normal for me. Received Drixoral plus EEG, brain scan and sinus x-rays. I was not asked about these tests, and was very surprised when the EEG technician arrived in my room.

Nov. 18th

Bone marrow biopsy, results normal, WBC's had dropped to 3.6. No cause found. CBC, Electrolytes.

Nov. 21st

Could go home but chose to wait for cysto and go without Foley.

Nov. 25th

Cysto & dilation, woke up without Foley. On Cysto, bladder was hypertonic and had some thickening at meatus from Foleys. EKG, serum steroids

Nov. 26th

Dolores admitted to Hospital (also) for incision and drainage of perianal abcess., staph. I was able to visit her.

Nov. 27th

Dolores discharged home.

Nov. 28th

Discharged home, no Foley no caths since cysto.

Dec. 8th

Peter's parents cancelled their visit.

Dec. 26th

Holiday in East, Peter HAD to go to work. Admitted to Hospital with concussion. Skull series, EEG. Ba enema and sigmoid which Dr. B had wanted before. I did not see any reason for this but wanted to cooperate.

Jan. 1st

Hospital since 26th. Headaches following concussion from fall at home on outside steps. *Cause not known.*

Jan. 12th

Dr. Berent.

Jan. 16th

Returned to work. Dr. Berent, Psychotherapy explained to me and all of my questions answered. The situation was very strange to me and I was not sure that I could respond in the manner required for successful treatment.

Bladder improving at home.

Jan. 21st

Optometrist

Jan.

Dr. Berent, 22nd, 26th, 27th, 30th.

Feb.

Dr. Berent, 2nd, 3rd, 4th, 5th, 9th, 10th, 11th. 12th having some difficulty in therapy

Feb. 17th

Dr. B, CBC.

Feb. 19th

Dr. Berent, I forgot about my app. with him, there are so many to keep that I can't make it everywhere.

Feb. 20th

Dr. Berent.

Feb. 25th

7:30 A.M. My employee physical, thyroid nodule found, advised to see Dr. B. 9:40 A.M. Dr. Berent.

Feb. 27th

Left work after 4 hrs., with severe nausea and vomiting.

Mar. 1st

Dr. B, Thyroid scan ordered.

Mar. 2nd

Thyroid scan, cold nodule, heard tecs. talking and knew what it was. 9:40 Dr. Berent.

Mar. 4th

Dr. Berent.

Mar. 8th

Dr. B for surgery consult.

Mar. 9th
>   Dr. W, surgery decided.

Mar. 16th
>   Hospital pre-op.

Mar 17th
>   Sub Total Thyroidectomy, nodule benign.
>   Dolores Chickenpox.

Mar. 18th
>   9 P.M. sudden T 104 chills, cough. Dr. W in, Blood cultures, chest x-ray, I.P.P.B. Hypothermia X 24 hrs. Diagnosis, pylonephritis.

Mar. 26th
>   Discharged.

Mar. 30th
>   Dr. Berent.

Apr. 5th
>   Sam T. 103-104? Chickenpox.

Apr. 6th
>   Dr. Berent.

Apr. 7th
>   Sam—Chickenpox! T 104.

Apr. 8th
>   Dr. Berent.

Apr. 9th
>   Dr. B.

Apr. 11th
>   Sam very sick, T104, 105. lying in bed sleeping most of the time X 3 days. Dr. F, Chickenpox with secondary infection.

Apr. 12
>   Dr. W, check, OK. Sam improving.

Apr.
>   Dr. Berent 13th. 15th.

Apr. 19th
>   Sam, has abcess on shoulder, staph, Prostaphillin.

Apr. 20th
>   Dr. Berent. Interview at University Hospital.

Apr. 22nd
>   Dr. Berent

Apr. 27th
>   4 day Critical Care Symposium.

May 3rd
>   Dr. Berent. Returned to work post surgery.

May 5th
>   Hospital interview and physical.

May 6th
>   Dr. Berent.

May 10th
>   Started at University Hospital. Orientation, professional testing, ICU certification, etc.

May 26th
>   Dr. Berent.

May 28th
>   Dr. B.

Jun. 3rd
>   Arrythmia test at U. Hospital.

Jun.
>   Dr. Berent, 15th, 22nd.

Jul.
>   Dr. Berent, 6th., 15th.

Jul. 17th
>   AACN test Critical Care Certification.

Jul. 22nd
>   Dr. B. sinusitis, erythromycin.

Jul. 26th
>   Sam. staph, erythromycin. Dr. Berent. I decided to end therapy, wished to cope normally.

Aug.
>   Normal month. Felt well.

Sept. 8th
>   Dr. Berent, made appointment to see because of feeling just not quite right, but nothing that could be named.

Sept. 14th
>   Dr. Berent, 16th, 23rd, 28th.

Oct. 1st

Dr. Berent. Now feeling more relaxed. Thought that the need to see Dr. Berent was just transitional from finishing therapy.

The children were having problems, Sam, croup with impending hospitalization for a few hrs., but he recovered after a few watchful nights. Sam was born with Laryngo-malacia but this was the only time that he was threatened with a real problem.

Oct. 5th

Dolores, strep, throat, penicillin X 10 days.

Oct.

Following some busy satisfactory days at work, I recall that I was fatigued by the end of the day. I left home at 6:10 A.M. start at 7 A.M. There were many days in this period that I worked late. This caused guilt and anger. Anger when I left late because of prolonged time in giving nursing report; this I thought unnecessary and resulted in me being late to pick children up at school. Often late [and guilty] because emergencies are an accepted part of an ICU nurse.

It was a struggle to keep up with all of my tasks. I had no problems at work but was very tired in the evenings. This I realized not fair to Peter or the children. I gave a lot of thought to changing my work schedule but this was not possible at the time because MICU was a new unit. And doing well, I felt that I owed it loyalty and consideration. Therefore, I continued as I was, with hopes that things would be better in the future. There was one new problem. In about 2 weeks I was due to do 1 mths night rotation. I was worried about this and did not know how I would handle it [with previously described poor sleeping during the day].

During this time I had a feeling that all was not well but because of the above problems, I believed that I could ride it through.

I told Peter that I did not feel good. He wanted me to stop work and suggested that I see Dr. Berent but I most of all wanted to live normally, cope with life's problems.

Oct. 20th

Peter talks about the two previous nights when I kept going out into the garden late at night. I can only recall that it was one night. He also states that I took too many baths.

I remember going out into the garden, I had a feeling that I wanted to escape. There was no where to go and that was not "realistic" but going into the garden relieved some of my restricted feelings and was a harmless way to deal with them. I felt trapped when Peter insisted that I stayed in; at one time I managed to slip out for a few mins. and swing on the children's swing. I came in feeling much better.

The baths, I have frequently taken a bath when unable to sleep or in the past when I had bladder problems. I realized that I had taken one, and repeated them on one night, but I was becoming tired of Peter's questions and told him that I did not remember that I had just taken one. I felt that I did not have to explain to anyone.

Oct. 20th

Normal busy day at work.

My recollections start that eve. where I was collecting pictures of the children and something religious and leaving them on my bed. I don't recall any feelings other than I needed them to be close.

I remember it being 7 P.M., the children were in bed, it was my day off the next day. And, although I don't recall any plans to take medication, it must of been in my mind somewhere because Peter walked in just when I had finished a note to U. Hospital. I left it for him to find so that he would pick up my pay check which was due the next day, my day off. Peter questioned this because normally I would wait until I was at work (the following day) to pick it up. I believe that I put him off by telling him that I needed it.

Oct 20th-21st cont.

Next I remember going to say goodnight to my children. Sam was asleep, I remember being disappointed about this. Dolores was awake. I told her how much I loved her and asked her if she loved me; she responded with a kiss and cuddle. Next I asked her to promise me something, that she would never become a nurse. At that time I recall a feeling of hopelessness and an urgency to do something about it. Peter was already suspicious.

I remember clearly taking the Dalmane and a glass of water

into the library, out of Peter's sight. I counted 6 capsules into my hand and put the rest back into the bottle. I had a sense of fear and swallowed them quickly before I lost my nerve.

Peter came into the room just after I had taken them. After his threats, I realized what I had done and told him that I had only taken 6 and would be able to sleep it off. At this stage he did not believe me and called Dr. Berent who advised ER and for Peter to call rescue if he could not talk me into going.

I did not want to go. I believe there was no need, no one would believe me. Rather than call rescue, I went to ER unwillingly. I was becoming increasingly angry. At ER I was given the usual medication to cause vomiting. Then sent home. I did not want to stay there and yet I did not want to go home, perhaps I was still angry. I was unsteady on my feet and had to leave in a wheelchair; *no one had asked me how I felt.*

At home Peter set the alarm for each hr. to check that I was awake, he slept in between. I was wide awake the whole time and after about 3 hrs. told him to forget it. He did because it was obvious that I was wide awake. I did not have any intentions of taking any more medications at that time.

I do not recall any *plan* to take more medication. I was wide awake thinking a lot and thought that I have been treated unfairly in that no one would believe in me. In one sudden decision in a hurry again whilst I had the courage, I remembered some Nembutal put away out of the children's reach. I made sure that Peter was asleep and quickly counted out 6 capsules putting the remainder away.

I recall getting up in the morning and telling Peter that I did not feel good. Peter said that I stumbled and that he caught me and put me back to bed. He had aroused me with a wet towel.

I was taken to ER by rescue later that morning. Peter did not have the experience to recognize a coma. He could only go by the Dr.'s response on the telephone and was reluctant to take me back because I had been to ER once and discharged. Peter thought that I was sleeping off the Dalmane.

Oct. 23rd

Remember being told by nurse that it was 1 A.M. and that I was in Hospital ICU and that I was on a respirator and should keep my hands still because I had I.V.'s. I did not think about this or question anything. I don't believe that I was awake enough to; or that I thought I was dreaming.

My next recollection was hearing Peter telling me that I had been asleep for a long time and that he, Dolores, and Sam loved me and wanted me to get better. He also told me that my sister was there. I did know then everything they said. But, I was unable to communicate back to them because of the respirator and also because my eyes were out of focus. I could not write.

Peter put my hand into his and I remember that I did not squeeze it because I felt angry with him. To me, it was like the next morning and we had an unresolved argument of the night before, which I felt that we had to talk over to be friends again.

I had no sensation of the time, or of all that had passed. The first reality that hit me was that I was not going to be able to go to work that day. I made many attempts to communicate to the nurse that she call U. Hospital before 5 A.M., the time that you call in sick by.

At about 8 A.M. I was extubated then made a rapid recovery. I was not allowed to see Peter for about 5 hrs. after extubation because of a Code Blue that lasted at the most 2 hrs. Also, I had just been given a bath and left very cold with just a sheet on until Peter came in and asked for a blanket for me. I could not shout at the time and had no call light.

Oct. 24th

Awake and alert, was told that I could be out of ICU but would have to stay because it was Sunday. I should of insisted at this point. I must of been a bit lethargic to go along with it. The nurses later that day told Peter that I had no right being there. It sure did not help me—to feel so wanted!

Oct. 25th

Awake have had no sleep since I came out of coma, still have not put things together, nothing seems real, need more time to think. A Neurologist and Dr. K said Hi: then, that they were going to sign off the case. I had not had time to think of any questions to ask them at the time.

Drs. Berent and E. visited over the weekend, both were very nice but looked worried. Dr. B visited, I thought that he would answer all the questions which I had by then collected. Instead, he told me and everyone else in ICU just what he thought of me. He asked me questions but did not allow me to reply, instead he answered them with his own answer.

I was told that nothing need of happened and that nothing was necessary. I, under this verbal abuse before I was ready for it, forgot to ask pertinent questions like my present medical condition and possible discharge. Then, with time to reflect, I had to make my own decision and decided to leave where I was told I was not wanted, that was something I could do without.

That morning, being more awake, I noticed from the pain and headache it caused a large hematoma on my head, occipital area, it felt like it had been lacerated and I could feel dried blood in my hair. Which I later washed out at home.

I must note that a hematoma that large should not of been missed in a coma patient. I was offered EEG, skull series and an EMI, but it was a bit late after recovery from a coma.

Oct. 27th

Dr. Berent called because of headache and not doing well at home. Admitted to Psych. Hosp. Unable to cope with problems of new house, discharged after 4 days. Continuing to see Dr. Berent as an outpatient.

One Patient 11th Dec. 197—.

Comments About "the Record"

As the patient and I focused on her notes which concretely illustrated to both of us what I had previously suggested—namely, being gradually eroded and *overwhelmed* primarily by medical events—she began to fill in some of the flashing feelings that had been "forgotten." Most pertinent was clarification of the "amnesia" regarding *falling down steps* 10 days before my very first consultation with her. It had not been just an accident, such as slipping or "the cat perhaps jumping at me." In retrospect, she now could recall sensations of wishing her death as she stood at the top of the stair landing. Although her physicians did not recognize her suicide attempt, they responded to certain other symptoms and obtained her reluctant consent to consult with a psychiatrist. Our earlier meetings never did clear up the mystery of the stairs. Possibly, "the cat may have startled me" was accepted as explanation enough for the accident. Therapists, too, just as other humans, would rather not have to look at the gross feelings of suicide. It is much easier to accept the idea of a less life-or-death issue, such as psychologically induced bladder retention. In all fairness to my diagnostic acumen, I must relate to the reader that as part of my commentary to the patient indicating empathy with her frequent bouts of illness, I did stress on more than one occasion that she must have been extremely depressed when so burdened and perhaps could have had moments of wishing to be dead. Such remarks would be met with some welling up of tears but no further frank admissions.

Our meetings continued to focus on her responses to current and past illnesses, which, in spite of our efforts, were being inflicted continually upon her by the Fates to the point of inundating her. As she seemed to indicate in her diary, meetings with me were taking on the character of just additional medical meetings, all of which she would have wished to discard. Beginning with her vaginal hemorrhages (and subsequent hysterectomy) and father's death, further less intense events were being experienced as additional onslaughts upon her spirit. Her energies, already spread to cover roles as nurse, mother, wife, and grieving daughter, were limited and no match for the many incessant drops of stimuli constituting the erosion process.

Again, the reader might take particular notice of the patient's retrospective notes covering the two to three days prior to the second suicide attempt. She describes going out at night into the garden and, on one occasion, swinging in the children's swing. Already, she was envisioning the "freedom" of death. No longer would she be pressed by her work and illnesses. Death would be a release from the confines of responsibility. In fantasy, death would restore to her long lost days of carefree existence, regressively symbolized by her being gently carried and nurtured in her children's swing.

When other suicidologists refer to the period in which the depressed person suddenly looks better as being dangerous in suicide potential, they are referring to the above state which has occurred through the final ushering in of fantasy. The suicidal person, not having found a sufficient rescuer in real life and now being completely overwhelmed, turns death into the ultimate rescuer, with a sense of relief.

In concluding this chapter, I wish once again to stress and underline how overwhelming crisis could be pictured as mobilizing fantasy at the expense of reality. What we must do for our suicidal patient in restoring a sense of reality might be dramatically portrayed by the content of a cartoon I saw many years ago. My not saving it probably related to initially being repelled by it. However, the message is very apt. Basically, the cartoon portrays a patient lying on the proverbial couch with his analyst sitting behind him. However, the viewer's eyes rivet on a rope held in the analyst's hand that runs above and attaches to a guillotine poised directly over the patient's head. The caption to the cartoon has the analyst saying, "Compared to *this,* what are your problems!?''

There might be many ways to interpret this cartoon. However, to me, the essence is the preciousness of life that we tend to forget and minimize when caught up in our problems and fantasies. Indeed, fantasies have an ability to make us oblivious to the fact that dead is dead. The suicidal patient, like the person in the described cartoon, needs to have his awareness reestablished as to the significance of his suicide action. It would not lead to a death in which fantasies can be played out and enjoyed. Instead, his fantasies would have mobilized an act in which he would be ushered into nothingness.

Chapter 5

CHRONIC SUICIDER

Chronic suicider is a term I am using to depict a person utilizing a process or processes that may gradually lead to suicide. Some individuals may seem arrested somewhere along the process just short of death and be suspended in limbo for what would appear to be eons. Others, where the balance gives way, precipitously drive themselves to their ultimate solution. I have intentionally used the word *drive* to also refer to those automobile accidents that might well have been suicides. Indeed, other writers have used the term chronic suicider to refer to such people. Also, this category may include those who drink themselves to death. Drug users and people who exhibit other self-destructive behaviors have likewise been included in this category. The following constructs are part of the total picture.

AMBIVALENCE

Ambivalence, a psychiatric term, is an important and useful concept within which we can speak further about the chronic suicider. A cartoon depicting patient and analyst condenses the meaning of ambivalence well: "I could never come to terms with the intense, unresolved ambivalent feelings I had for that horrible, demoniac, overpossessive wretched mother of mine who used to do all those wonderful, kind and thoughtful things for me!" The patient struggles with the simultaneous wishes of longing for mother's attentions and services while being repulsed by the feeling of being once more in her power as a child—and then hating her possessiveness. We just can't have it both ways! To indulge ourselves in the little girl or boy role with the parent nourishing in all ways we must, by definition, partake of its other ramifications—being controlled like a little child. There's the rub! And yet the longing may persist.

This leads to another concept, that of *conflict*: the presence of simultaneous yet opposing wishes or desires. As mentioned earlier, our primitive beginnings depend upon our being "magically" cared for. When all goes well, "good" parents exist (and vice-versa). We are loved; we love. If parents miss our cues, they are hated; we are hated. A later chronological manifestation of this phenomenon is the adolescent who wants all the privileges of an adult but is not willing to let go of his more childish desires and benefits, therefore making it impossible to accept the responsibilities of the adult position. Again, the outward show of this conflict may present as hating or loving. We are loving when we feel loved; hating when we feel hated. That these several feelings may go on simultaneously is common knowledge. Implications of this phenomenon are important and subtle, affecting dramatically the relationships individuals form.

In "normal" amount, these back and forth expressions of feeling reflect usual development, par for the course. In excessive amount, various pathological offshoots arise. The suicidal person is a case in point, for excessive ambivalence frequently colors the attitude shown by such a person at the time of overwhelming crisis. *Loving* or *hating* may be paralleled with *living* or *dying*. Some examples of ambivalence as applied to suicide follow.

The dramatic scene of the would-be suicidal person on the roof of a tall building threatening to jump, with a policeman, fireman, or clergyman inching his way to the potential victim, is a striking image. We are often impressed by what seems to be such a paradox—someone wanting to die, yet leaving the possibilities open for rescue. As the rescuer comes closer the victim threatens to jump. It becomes a back and forth "game" in which the outcome may or may not be fatal. The rescuer has to emanate vibrations of concern and yet not move too fast or suddenly for fear the victim will jump. On the other hand, the rescuer cannot move too slowly, either, lest the victim interpret this as a form of rejection and phony interest. The rescuer is an externalized symbol to the victim —a conglomeration of the important people in his past and present life. How he moves, what he says, the tone of his voice all contribute to whether the potential victim visualizes the "good" parents or "bad" ones in his head. Briefly, we could imagine some of the following with our potential victim: Is the would-be rescuer condescending or natural? Scolding or concerned? Making the victim ashamed or giving some face-saving alternatives? And on and on. In spite of all attempts, however, the main action is going on in the head of the potential victim and may truly be *almost* completely independent of the rescuer. "Does he love me or doesn't he love me?" often being a reflection of "do I love or hate?" What are the pictures that come to mind?

A clinical situation may further illustrate ramifications of ambivalence. Mr. Z, the same 60-year-old man I mentioned in the CUSS section, was referred also because of depression and exasperation over various physical infirmities. As the reader may recall, a long history of medical complaints included high blood pressure and difficulty in bowel movements for which he had engineered a regime of large fluid intake resulting in episodes of marked urination that seemingly stimulated greater success in defecation. However, shortly after forced retirement was brought about by certain external circumstances beyond his control, the patient had an intensification of physical symptoms, including several episodes of convulsions as well as pains in his legs, which he further described as having become ugly by engorged veins. In the past year, he had been hospitalized several times at a competent university but, according to his physician, with minimum objective findings. Even his high blood pressure would quickly reduce itself to normal levels.

However, the patient's concerns continued unabated. Indeed, the crescendo of symptoms, now including "his prostate gland and testicles," had the patient pleading for additional hospitalization and becoming angry with his physician for no longer complying with his desires. At the time of my finally seeing him, he had decided to dismiss his regular physician, who, he felt, no longer was concerned with him. He beseeched me to refer him to another physician who might appraise his physical conditions from a "fresh point of view," and I complied. As soon as he had received his additional consultations, he found himself angry with the new physician, whose evaluation was basically similar to that obtained from his former physician. However, since hospitalization for further diagnostic studies was agreed to by the new physician, the patient was being half-hearted in his responses to him.

Upon my going to visit him in the hospital, I was met by his nurses who exclaimed, "Thank God you've come to see him! He's so cantankerous, like a bear. Nothing pleases him. He's sarcastic and nasty." During our visit (and reflecting on several others we had in my office) it became clear that his seeming obnoxiousness was a cover for underlying panic and anxiety regarding his physical state. He had become convinced the Fates had let him down and that no doctor or nurse could stop the degenerative changes that rapidly would have him in his grave. "I might as well swallow some pills and be done with it!" As we talked further certain other misconceptions that had contributed to his panic became clear. He had consulted a urologist regarding his bladder, prostate, and testicles and was told that no surgical intervention was necessary. However, he construed the physician's attempt to underscore the possibility that his symptoms were psychological as really saying: "You need the operation, but your mental state would not allow you to survive the procedure."

Rather than being reassured about his physical state and concentrating on the mental state that was fueling many of his somatic complaints, the patient became increasingly agitated. He had further complicated the picture by alienating his spouse and children by providing an erroneous picture of the physician's conversation with him. They thought the patient was refusing an operation that would be helpful and, incidentally, spare them hearing repetitive renditions of his troubles. An argument ensued, the patient had another convulsion; high blood pressure and other complaints once again were at new heights; and the patient had to be hospitalized for evaluation.

All this information could be obtained only after some relief from his basic fright and panic by my bypassing his negative-aggressive behavior: "Look, Mr. Z, I think you're acting this way because you're scared stiff! Now let me hear what you've been told once again!" Fortunately, I had been in touch with his other physician and knew the facts. These could now be contrasted with some of his distortion, and some measure of relief obtained.

This long story highlights the near tragic consequences a combination of ambivalence and panic may provide. Under the influence of anxiety and panic, the patient may not comprehend what is told him by his consultant. Complicated by his ambivalence in which he tends to react with anger, he drives away just the individuals who might otherwise try to again reassure him. Until the superficial crusts of his problem are penetrated, the underlying emotional fuels remain providing their heat and discomfort. Elaboration of these areas becomes the next order of business, to fully aid him in dealing with his depressions and tendencies to convert many emotional feelings into bodily ones. Several times he had been brought to a "rescuer," only to feel rejected ultimately as a response to his own output of negative vibrations. Since both physicians and family members were becoming impatient with him, the potential for suicide was rapidly increasing at the time of his initial psychiatric consultations.

Another example in which the concept of ambivalence may be seen operating is the anonymous caller. In speaking to individuals who have attended hotlines one hears frequently of such a person. The person rapidly makes it clear that he is considering suicide but will not give his name, location, and so on. In spite of properly given encouragement, he will not consent to come to the clinic and yet may call periodically for months or years. The tendency toward distant relationships is well epitomized by such an individual, literally and figuratively. The thread holding him to life is so thin. What can also be so exasperating to the rescuer is that the suicide person is seemingly seeking help but does not accept it when it is offered. Basically, the rescuer is not being given the chance to rescue. The obvious danger is for the rescuer to become impatient and incensed at such a caller, feeling that he is just having his time wasted.

A number of years ago, I was consulted by an older man who described visualizing round smothering balls larger and larger before his eyes to the point of being almost hypnotized by them. In exchange for telling his story, he wished that I would prescribe Miltown for him; he said that he knew the medication would help him, since he had received the same medication from a physician years before in another city—he felt liked by the doctor. Professing small income, he declined further consultations, but hoped I would continue prescribing the drug in the future should he call. There was no convincing him that he should have additional consultations with me. His story had been related as intimately as he chose to give it. He had left Europe alone as a teenager to go to South Africa, where a distant relative was to teach him the jewelry trade. This accomplished, he came to America, where he has supported himself as a watch repairman. All through this narration, his story was marked by its absence of other important human beings. Certainly an aura of mystery was conveyed, not so much by intention, but rather as a result of an empty life.

The importance of this example is that the man has kept a thin thread of connection to me during these past dozen years by periodically having his pharmacist call to request a refill of his Miltown. The fine thread continues as he wards off his more dependent wishes. The link to his doctor (through the Miltown) represents his rescue. This is not ordinarily good medicine from the physician-rescuer ideal point of view (and a patient on medication of this sort should have periodic blood checks). There is frustration on my part, pangs of conscience; my role as a ''proper'' physician has been compromised. In a sense I am similar to the person on the hotline who cannot get the phone caller to come in or identify himself. Again, this is an illustration of someone wanting contact and fearing it at the same time. Thinking there must be something else we might do, we question the value of our endeavors, wishing to do much more. Yet limitations exist. As in other branches of medicine, there are conditions that we cannot actually cure. We can alleviate some of the complaints, but that may be the best we can do. In general medicine, we are more apt to accept such resignations. However, it is increasingly difficult to do so with emotional situations. Indeed the rescuer does have conflict over the method of pulling the patient closer without frightening the patient away completely with too much expressed concern or pressure (like the rescuer trying to save the victim on the roof). To second guess the mind of the ambivalent person remains constantly a confusing task. But where there is doubt, let me reassure the reader that the better position is one of activity—try to make the rescue. A patient describing a previous psychiatric exposure that was interrupted by two years military service said that he felt the former therapist had "dropped the ball" when he did not insist that his patient return to him upon completion of service. What this insistence would have had to be may be another story. At any rate, "the ball was dropped" certainly meant a sense of rejection at the least. As explored with this patient, the sense of rejection may be something that he inadvertently sets up as if to claim some type of mastery over the sensation. If one does not expect much, an acute sense of disappointment may be avoided. It is the *acute* sense of painful disappointment that is warded off. Yet, *chronic* disappointment has to be the alternative created by the defenses that ward off the acute pain.

DEPENDENCE

Dependence, another psychiatric term, refers to a concept that often characterizes the chronic suicider and has been alluded to above. The movie actress who claims she does not know what she will be thinking about today because her analyst is out of town is a little joke that makes the point with hyperbole. Hopefully, her analyst will make her dependence a number one topic of future discussions. At any rate, dependency exists outside of the psychiatrist's office and most often in much more tense and destructive forms.

Closely related to ambivalence, as we will see, dependence originates in that earliest period of life, described in the Introduction, when the self (and its parts) is fused with the mother (or father). Rather than having a normally progressive separation and individualization in growing up, certain individuals have an unevenness in development in which they are too stuck and intertwined with their old positions of magically expecting the parent (or the current-day substitute) to provide. As the individual grows chronologically older, the arrest in development becomes more apparent and the others in the surrounding world are less and less likely to perform in their scheduled roles. The obviously dependent person who is only chronologically getting older will gradually stir anger in those whom he or she has manipulated for survival. Constrastingly, in the beginning, such a dependent person might be experienced by a would-be rescuer as cute—for example, the actress of the preceding joke. This apparent defenselessness may have some type of appeal for certain other individuals whose own needs are flattered by being so important to the dependent individual. And such a relationship might continue for a number of years if the needs of both are being mutually (though neurotically) fulfilled. However, one example of such a relationship falling apart might serve to convey the potential tragedy built into it.

A woman in her late thirties brought herself to a psychiatric hospital stating that she just had to be admitted or she would commit suicide. Her appearance of being so distraught brought immediate response from the nurse in charge, who contacted the necessary physicians with subsequent arrangement for admission. At this moment in time, the patient had acted as her own rescuer. (She had brought herself to the hospital.) Shortly afterwards the husband came to the hospital and together they briefed the psychiatrist in charge about the circumstances leading to the crisis. What follows may leave the reader with the feeling that he or she is being exposed to the history of a spoiled brat rather than learning more about individuals who may commit suicide and the clues or cries for help that are given. Yet, it is exactly this attitude of spoiled brat that finally taints the reaction of would-be rescuers in certain instances and that allows the suicide victim no other recourse but to end life. So, however we might label certain persons, it will not alter the life course. We cannot by our labeling or sarcasm do away with the dejected, empty sensations of the would-be suicide person. Nor can we continually coddle such persons.

The above patient was born of extremely wealthy parents and raised as a "princess," being exposed to all the right social experiences and education of her station. Upon the death of her father when she was in her teens, her mother chose to take the family to an entirely different part of the world. Not only had she lost her father, but she had also lost her peers, her place in life, the many servants—all the trimmings and trappings of a young princess. However, the mother managed to place her daughter in a select girls' school, followed by the appropriate college. Seemingly the girl adjusted and evidenced no apparent severe psychological problems. But as explained in an earlier case, the child may remain an *emotional* child, with areas of deficit, while simultaneously acquiring skills that appear parallel to the age-specific attainments of others—especially in the protected environment of school.

Shortly after graduation and working part time for a couple of years, she married a man who was intrigued by her exotic background and was able to experience her dependence as further manifestations of her allure or cuteness. As life progressed, the woman was able to recreate the world of the past by her parties, teas, and benefits to which she could wear her more glamorous clothes. Her husband provided well, just as her father before. However, the bubble of this fairy-tale burst when she heard that her husband was interested in another woman. The years after marriage had brought further development and rewards for her husband in his business activities; he felt himself increasingly creative, with interesting people around him, equally talented and mutually stimulating. His wife, meanwhile, although skilled and intelligent, had remained essentially dormant, living out the reveries of "princess" without being able to keep pace with her husband's needs for companionship of a more mature nature. When confronted with the "other woman," the patient sought solace from others, including her family and friends, but to no avail as far as bringing her husband around. Playing on his guilt also failed to reestablish her sole position of princess—he acknowledged that he still cared for her (almost in terms of a child) and hoped that the hospitalization would motivate her to search for more rewarding interests that could also increase his respect for her.

In spite of this stimulus for growth, the patient found it extremely difficult to alter her personality, even with the attention of hospital staff and psychiatrist. At each interpretation of her little girl position, she would recoil or ask that she have a different therapy or group or doctor. When some of these changes were made, it was more apparent than ever that she continued to inspire the same reactions in the new people who were to be her therapists. And then the process would be repeated—"I want a new group" or "I want a new doctor." The tenacity with which she fought to maintain her dependent style of action (not really knowing any other) was remarkable to the uninitiated. Frustrating to those who wanted to help her was the knowledge that the hospitalization was now being used to sanctify her dependence, calling it an illness (which it is, actually), and to help her in the endeavors to win back her husband's interest without really facing up to the characteristics that got her in this situation in the first place. It was a holding action, giving her time and space. Whether or not the patient subsequently was able to emerge into more mature roles was to determine her eventual outcome. But that she had come to the "end of her rope" at the time of her admission to the hospital, there was no doubt. One would hope that her therapist could maintain a push upon her, without making her flee. Also that he would not find himself giving up on her, as he fights the neurotic core that stands in the way of her blossoming into a more substantial person. The themes of therapy for any one patient may not be that many; however, the patience needed by both the patient and the therapist to relive some of the feeling tones and eventually make modifications is necessarily great. The time spent can be long. Cynicism of others regarding favorable outcome is also understandable in the face of extreme persistence of the old and familiar life style that does not change by just pushing a button.

POTENTIAL SECONDARY RESCUERS

Like the villagers who have heard the boy cry "Wolf" once too often, the prime rescuer (whether mother, father, spouse, etc.) may have "had it." Then what? The above clinical example represents a final, last-ditch point. What about the intervening situations? Who are some of the other individuals who might be placed in the role of rescuer for any one suicidal person?

THE NEIGHBOR. Mundane as it seems, the neighbor frequently has a good ear. The potential suicide victim may express and voice opinions that help clear the air (or give time to recover), restoring some equilibrium. Providing that this mechanism is not too abused or too one-sided, the safety-valve aspects may function well. If one wears out one's welcome, other possibilities will be required. That the neighbor may be the neighborhood bartender should not altogether surprise us in some cases! This theme is more than sufficiently portrayed in cartoons and jokes. But the truth remains. Such individuals may well function in this capacity for some of their clients, and also be safety-valves.

THE CHURCH OR CLUB GROUP. Frequently the clergyman is sought out for counseling. When the individual comes straight out with the area of conflicts, the chances of rescue are excellent. However, one should appreciate a particular feeling that certain persons have—namely, they do not want to upset their minister (or physician) with their troubles, and these individuals may be extremely subtle in conveying their true feelings. A short example will make the point.

I was called by the mother of a 12-year-old girl who had asked her mother to contact a psychiatrist. When the mother had asked the child whether she first would speak to her pediatrician, she received this reply: "Oh, no! I like him too much! I couldn't heap my shit on him!" But the psychiatrist has asked for it by choosing his profession in the first place. The story is accurate and strikingly highlights a warning: that certain would-be rescuers may receive only veiled emanations of disturbance from their patients, or congregation members, or friends and relatives, because of the respect and love they enjoy from the would-be seeker of help. It is not unusual for a patient to tell the psychiatrist at the first meeting numerous pertinent emotional facts that the referring doctor is just amazed to hear. "How did you ever get so much in just one meeting? I've known the patient for years!" The inference is that we have a crystal ball or just superb interview techniques. The fact that we are known to be psychiatrists has our role defined for us in the patient's eyes. The patient can "heap on the shit" to quote my 12-year-old patient. In more recent years, the role of clergyman has been expanded to include counseling, and to the degree that the seeker of help knows this, he can enjoy these services. Incidentally, in speaking with some clergymen who have functioned in the counseling capacity, they have spoken of instances where they have performed well in the capacity of rescuer only to lose the individual as a regular member of the congregation. It was just too embarrassing for the congregation member, and another church had to be sought out. Difficult? Yes, but better to have a live congregation member going to any church!

THE PHYSICIAN'S RECEPTIONIST OR NURSE. It is not uncommon at all for patients to split functions and roles. Like the 12-year-old girl mentioned above, many patients are too concerned about the feelings of their doctors: they do not want to burden him, take too much of his time, or run the risk of his disapproval. (This may be true for many other rescuers.) Thus, to relate emotions directly becomes forbidden. A corollary to this is the fact that the physician has *physical conditions* as his frame of reference, and patients are most flexible and adaptable (consciously or unconsciously) presenting their problems in the form of body symbolism. Indeed, a physical focus most frequently anticipates that not all is well in the world of the psyche for the patient. This was seen with Mr. Z above. Another shorter example with a different twist follows.

A patient sees a gastrointestinal specialist and speaks of frequent episodes of diarrhea in the mornings. After examination, which may include x-rays or sigmoidoscopic exams, is told that everything is O.K. Just a bit of nerves! "In fact, Mrs. S, I've got the same trouble!" That the woman's condition continues but with more obvious evidence of depression is a natural progression of her illness. That she finally sees a psychiatrist, in spite of her gastrointestinal physician, happens again to be part of a true story.

But the other cases do not necessarily proceed in this fashion. Instead, some very desperate patients will choose to tell only their doctor's secretaries or nurses of their emotional situations. These people will be chosen as rescuers. It is a wise physician (or clergyman) who, knowing this, will instruct all his staff to be attentive to this phenomenon and convey immediately to his attention anything that seems unusual about his patient's (or congregation member's) visit. His staff must not make the assumption that what Mrs. S tells them, she has already told the doctor. If this assumption is made, we have the same conditions being set up as those in which Mr. Y is shown the rope by Mr. X described earlier in the journal—everyone *assumes* the doctor will know. And the doctor is just another human being!

One of the earliest models for this split function where the physician has his role and his nurse receptionist her role is that of the family. Mother is home during the day. It is to her that one frequently goes with bruised knees or bruised feelings. Father has had a hard day at the office and should be spared some of the burdensome details of the day. We have had the model of split functions for years! But in contrast to our parents who (hopefully) did manage to speak together in the evening (and about us when necessary), our doctor and his staff may not ordinarily get together to sift out the emotions of their patients. It would be very unlikely on a day-to-day basis. Yet the old model of mother and father doing so may be an operative fantasy in the mind of the suicide person; the patient may feel rejected when not confronted by the physician, who *should* have known—almost like magic—what was conveyed to his office staff, and asked about the reasons for the tearfulness while waiting in the outer office.

SUMMARY

To summarize this section: the dependent woman described above, who was her own immediate rescuer in that she brought herself to the hospital pleading for admission, has most likely gone through all the other rescuers— neighbors, church groups, bridge groups, tea groups, doctors and their receptionists, and, most important of all, her husband. She has worn out her welcome. The 15 or so years of marriage to her husband has been a grind; he has seen her through many physical illnesses, crying spells, tiffs with relatives and himself. Her "clinging" has lost its appeal, to the point that when she says how desperate she is feeling, he tells her that he's through. He will not this time accompany her to any doctor, as he has done in the past. He's through, and she can take a "flying leap." And basically this was the quality of their conversation prior to her presenting herself to the hospital for admission. It truly was her last straw. All in all, such a person gets less and less positive responses, to the point of experiencing exaggerated desperation and alienation. She would have committed suicide were she not hospitalized. This does not mean that hospitalization is a cure-all, as plainly indicated above. But there are possibilities. How the external world responds to her is obviously important. As writers in the past have indicated about the suicide patient, his or her social circumstances help supply the setting in which the suicide act might take place. Yet, we must not forget the individual myth of the past (whether "princess" or some other) that may be operative in the suicide person currently. To illustrate the point let me enlarge on the princess myth. In current life, with her exaggerated dependency, she was reenacting the spirit of connection to the days prior to her father's death and her loss of familiar surroundings. Mystically, magically, and neurotically, she was attempting to create the aura of the past in her current relationships with people. But *now* they would not have it! As this dawns on her, she is once more bereft. Her sensation of isolation can only increase. Suicide as a last-ditch attempt at fulfilling her rescue (although in fantasy) becomes more and more possible. Only if a rescuer can aid her in comprehending the living actuality of her myth might there be hope in restoring her to new life. The myth is the necessary factor in any suicide. The social conditions provide secondary ingredients that may make the myth, or its failure, seem overwhelming. And such is the nature of crisis.

I would like to reemphasize that the overwhelming suicidal crisis may present in two forms. The more obvious might be the out and out *emotional,* as exemplified by the "princess" who gets herself admitted to a psychiatric hospital. By contrast, Mr. Z presented primarily with *physical* complaints and even was hospitalized in a general medical hospital. However, when we recognize that emotional problems may be the central core of certain presenting conditions, we may not be so surprised in retrospect to hear about certain suicides that have occurred in general hospitals. Again, old stereotypes let us imagine and accept suicides in *psychiatric* settings, but not in hospitals that treat people for physical diseases! Again, the myth or fantasy operating within the individual, whether he or she presents with emotional or physical problems, is the crucial issue in determining suicidal potential. When and if a real-life rescuer can be provided and accepted will be the essential turning point. Admittedly, to speak of *just* a rescuer may seem simplistic. This presents the "bottom line," to use sales jargon. The intervening steps that include specific wishes, hopes, or their symbolic equivalents sometimes expressed in somatic fashion together constitute individual myths that require elaboration in order to better comprehend what is wanted from the rescuer. Although one may not have the opportunity of knowing precisely the myth's content within a particular potential suicide victim's mind, the fact that one responds to something amiss already initiates the process of potential rescue. And, keeping such items as dependence and ambivalence in mind, one may persevere with rescue attempts in spite of meeting up with some resistance.

Chapter 6

DYNAMICS OF SUICIDE

In considering some of the dynamics of suicide, one must keep in mind continuously the *nature* of the state I am calling "overwhelmed." Characteristic of such a state is the presence of a set of phenomena often labeled "regression" or "repression." Or more colloquially expressed, being overwhelmed brings out the worst in us. What this means is that all the techniques, conscious and unconscious, that served us in some capacity in the years of growing up may be utilitzed at times of being overwhelmed. And many of these techniques are not very appealing when observed in grown individuals. Excessive fantasy, dependency, ambivalence, screaming, hating, brat-like behavior, sullenness, all may be most prominent at times of overwhelming crisis. Once more, this could lead to that erroneous assumption about the suicide person—namely, that he or she is unusually *immature* or possesses other negative qualities. This is not the case as a general rule. That it may be so with certain individuals *is* true—some examples of which I have already given. But even with these people, it is the desperation of their being overwhelmed that sometimes brings these characteristics to the surface. Such characteristics exist in all of us. At certain stages of our lives, we have all been dependent, screaming, babyish, hateful, and bombarded with *enough*, all of us will have our threshold broken, thus succumbing to terror, panic, depression, and would be capable of being suicidal. Thus, I hope my remarks in earlier chapters, as well as in this one and future chapters, will not lull the reader (and prospective rescuer) into a sense of safety when dealing with a more mature suicidal person who may be more subtle in his rescue pleas.

AGGRESSION INTERNALIZED

The general idea is that killing oneself simultaneously destroys the important others in one's life, the images of whom live within us. "You'll be sorry when I'm gone!" The implication is that the suicide victim (although now dead) somehow still will be able to float around and point fingers at the now sorrowful, grief-stricken survivors who should have treated him better when he was alive. Elaboration of this idea may convey greater conviction of its validity. Reflecting back on the four cartoons that accompanied the poster "Help Stamp Out Mental Health," the progression of conscious awareness ("I've had it"—in the swamp, the first-drawn cartoon) to the more primitve sensation ("something is engulfing me" in the fourth cartoon) becomes apparent. The person under stress regresses from a more conscious, integrated mental state to a more primitive, amorphous position by degrees. Anger, frustration, a flailing of the arms, symbolically, if not literally, accompany the overwhelmed suicidal person in his last desperate moments. Fates, God, parents, spouses, children—all have directly, indirectly, or together failed to provide rescue and should share the victim's lot!

Simultaneous with the above may yet appear another feeling tone condensed within the suicide act. Subliminally aware of his own increasing hate for those who have failed as rescuers, the suicide victim may experience himself as grotesquely hideous and therefore deserving of his fate. He should be punished, and the suicide accomplishes that, too. Perhaps related to this feeling tone might be the old saw that we supposedly remember only the good things about the dead. Is it possible the suicide person in finally making himself dead is trying to be remembered in good terms by the survivors? Perhaps. What does seem always definite, however, is the accusation of the survivors: I have been essentially good but deserved better treatment from the world.

Again, the "You'll be sorry when I'm gone!" is descriptive of the developmental stage embodying characteristics we unfortunately tend to attribute to the very immature personality. However, the feeling tone, although markedly camouflaged in most instances, exists to some degree even in the most sophisticated suicides. Conceivably, this may have application to even the suicide cancer victim, who might thus be berating the Fates, The world, or God (all derivatives of the earlier mother and father who should have provided more beneficially and spared him his affliction). In this instance, once again the cancer victim's body equals his parents. To be let down by his body is to be abandoned by the parents. If this seems farfetched, a slightly different emphasis might be brought to your attention. In discussing certain medical ailments, physicians may make the comment: "It's too bad one couldn't have chosen one's genes (or parents) a bit better." Admittedly, this is said partly in jest and partly with the awareness that heredity plays a certain role in some illnesses. On any conscious level where logic prevails, parents are not really being blamed for illnesses. However, in the emotional life, logic may often be cast to the winds—the genes, the parents have caused my Fate.

The concept "overwhelming" needs just a little more elaboration at this point in order to continue keeping the above comments in perspective and believable for the reader. Just prior to being overwhelmed and succumbing to the regressive phenomena, one is feeling pushed and pressured. More customary defenses are mobilized to put up a fight. The last-ditch stand is when all one's resources seem to have been utilized with nothing else left. All realistic (more mature) forms of protection have been employed, and yet we are still going under. At such a time, people turn to prayers. "Holy *Mother, Father in* heaven!" Not only is this a religious appeal, but it is also a revival of the archaic hopeful magical appeal to those earliest rescuers of our distress—Mom and Dad. And if we are to succumb to being overwhelmed, they haven't helped either! In our sense of abandonment, when subsequent energies are somehow transiently amassed, we may then hate and feel vengeful as we are being inundated by our crisis. We'll draw them down with us. In this sense, we might summarize and say that for every suicide, there is a homocide. Does this sound so stark? If so, let me quote the last lines of Mr. X's journal: "You know I am going to die. *I was standing by the window half an hour. I was waiting for you to come but you did not come.* Now I have finished with my life. God be with you. Goodbye. To whomever will be responsible after this: *I am pleading for the law to punish the sinners.* This is my last wish. Mr. X" The last desperate plea to his wife goes unanswered, with the subsequent sense of rage that she, a sinner, should be punished closing his thoughts and his life. He is a suicide and would-be homicide. Those of you who still remain skeptical reflect a few moments on newspaper reports in which the person takes the life of a dear one and then kills himself. He puts into literal homicidal action that which the patients above do in a symbolic sense. Certain statistical studies would seem to indicate that as many as one-third of suicides have committed an actual murder(s) as a preceding act! Here, too, there is seen to be a continuum and a fine line that separates symbolic action from the deed itself. A secondary factor that is also involved in some of these suicide-homicide events, especially when the homicide victim is a child, is the factor of identification. Basically, the child is frequently seen as an extension of the self. To the degree the suicidal person feels the child thinks and is a carbon copy of himself, it is beyond the comprehension of such a person to think that the child would not also wish to be dead. Only a "heartless" person would allow his child to live under such circumstances! Without a mother (or father) how could the child wish to live! As one could surmise, other ingredients, too, are intermeshed that may lead to the same horrendous result. For example, the child (or children) may be hated because of the additional strains and demands placed on an already overburdened parent. Or the suicide-homicide person may be doing to the child what he perceives to have been done to him (or her). Numerous ghoulish variations exist. All this is to indicate that the suicidal person is also a homicidal person—latent or actual.

The factor of identification, just like the factors of ambivalence and dependence illustrated in the previous chapter, has a remarkable influence during periods of overwhelming crisis. In contrast to ambivalence and dependence, the processes of identification may seem rather mystical, uncanny, and belonging to the realm of the supernatural rather than actually conveying much insight into the subject of suicide. At the risk of magnifying this impression, I would like the reader to consider yet another true clinical situation—an exaggerated one—to better comprehend the matrix in which the suicidal action (or homicidal action) takes place.

A woman arrived in my office after having phoned for an appointment and citing depression as the main problem. Upon my opening the door to the waiting room, I was met by one of the most battered individuals I had ever seen. Arm in a sling, black and blue areas over her legs, old linear scars on her arms; she described a motorcycle accident the previous weekend. Her past history was filled with episodes of comparable self-destruction, the lurid details of which would match the wildest imagination of any reader. As we continued to talk, I would ask for certain details of *her* life and would be surprised how frequently she would give answers as if I had asked about her *mother's* life. At first I thought I had been misunderstood. But then I realized how intimately fused she was with her mother. Many of her earliest memories included severe beatings from her mother, who, she felt, had had her own problems. But in spite of hateful feelings, she also loved her mother. Similarly, she wanted to take care of her mother and, at other times, be cared for by her mother. Alternation of roles had been frequent in recent years. Attempts at separating from the mother included putting geographical distance between them. But then "peculiar" reactions would follow. The patient would find herself extremely lonely, perform a severe act of self-mutilation (often life threatening) requiring hospitalization, and effect (usually) a transient reconciliation with the mother.

When extremely lonely, she would find her body trembling and her mind confused. Her speech would alternate in moments from that of a little child to that of a grown woman. An unreal almost hypnogogic state of mind would be in existence as further punishment and would be obsessively self-inflicted. From the point of view of identification or fusion, we might speculate that loneliness called forth an overwhelming crisis, which in turn evoked the fantasy of reunification with mother in its most primitve model: to beat herself was to be with the mother who had repeatedly beaten her. The loneliness was ended, and her mother could be called subsequently (in reality) in order to provide "forgiveness." Understandably the story was getting rather old for the mother, and the patient, after a while, would have to make do with the mothering responses of nursing staff. Fearing that the mother would finally be angry at her more current hospitalizations, she had begun not to notify the mother of her whereabouts. Similarly, false names might be used at hospitalizations to further keep her mother from knowing what happened. Depending upon her length of recovery, the mother could be tormented (beaten?) with anxiety for days or weeks at a time. When finally contacted, like the woman at the beach who has lost her child and fears it has drowned, she verbally beats the patient. And the cycle is ready to go again.

The patient is both beater and beaten. She is both mother and daughter. Dynamically, she is both a suicide and a homicide. All this is simultaneous. The reader should appreciate that these identifications may go in all directions. Earlier, I described the suicide person who might kill his child. This formula would include such psychic possibilities as (1) the suicide-homicide person being the grown child inflicting punishment (death) on his parent (i.e., "Just wait till I grow big! I'll get even with you, parent!"—the implication being that the suicidal adult is now the grown child and his *real* child is the grown-small parent); and (2) the suicide-homicide person being his own parent, reenacting old beating scenes on the suicide person's child (himself as a child in fantasy).

I realize that much earlier in the book I had promised to stick to "normal" suicidal persons rather than speak of the bizarre for fear that the reader would construe suicide problems as belonging only to the "crazy" among us. You'll forgive me if I apologize by stating that the above case and formulations are exaggerations of possible dynamics in "normal" people if in the state of overwhelming crisis. Ambivalence, dependence, and identification, with their ramifications, contribute to the internal milieu of the mind. When mixed with aggression and frustration, violence resulting in death may well follow. Fantasies may have a mystical, ethereal quality. The actions produced, however, are real, starkly real.

ORIGINS OF AGGRESSION

Theorists have taken or spoken of two positions. One is the *instinctual*. The premise is that we are biologically given the rudiments of aggression (instinct) within our genes and chromosomes. As with other animals, such as tigers and lions, aggression is built into us from the first moments of conception. The task of our parents and educators is to "civilize the little beasts." All joshing aside, there is a lot to be said for this point of view. The second position certain theorists have espoused is that aggression is not instinctual but rather the result of *frustration* by the parents and educators. When wishes of the child are not gratified, rage and frustration follow. The child has just wanted to be loving but his needs were not completely met, thereby triggering the seeds of the aggressive process. The two theoretical points of view give rise (in their extreme) to possible contrasting attitudes:

INSTINCTUAL. Because of the biological inheritance, we must look for explanations of suicide somewhere within the genes. Some variation of the normal has occurred; some inborn error of metabolism. In the affected individuals, the threshold of control over the instincts is lowered, or the instincts of aggression are just too intense as compared to those of individuals born with the appropriate quality and quantity. Through some quirks of Fate, these abnormal aggressive instincts are bent and redirected upon the suicide person himself. Nothing could have been done! It tends to get the rescuer off the hook; we feel miserable when we have missed our messages. It might be a relief to take this position and there may be some truth to it.

AGGRESSION SECONDARY TO FRUSTRATION. The extreme position could infer that suicide is the result of excessive frustration, that an individual need only be treated kindly and all will be well. The suicidal person has been entirely a victim of circumstances. It has not really been his fault, and the outer world is to be blamed.

Further details as to where responsibility lies will be deferred for several chapters. Meanwhile, to get back to a pragmatic point of view rather than spending more time with the theoretical, we might picture the situation as follows. Aggression, whether obtained from the moment of conception or from the frustrations of growing up and being properly educated, is translated first into thoughts and images about people and often contained well within our minds rather than always being channeled into acts. We have all had thoughts of wanting to kill someone but have kept the lid on. Some of us have had thoughts of killing ourselves, have considered the idea, but only fleetingly. Whether we have the instinct of aggression or not, we do know sensations that have contributed to feeling tones of sadness, futility, disillusionment, idealism that have gone awry. Certain of these memories remain within us and can be mobilized in moments. Disappointment is only a few steps away from rage and depression. It's all there. But under usual circumstances, our equilibrium is maintained by the balance of positive experiences which for the most part we take for granted. For the person whose balance seems to be tottering or who is too likely to be interpreting current opportunities through the jaundiced eyes of yesteryear, therapy may be most crucial. And the aggressions (and depressions) are most likely to be contained by such prophylactic therapy measures. The general treatment plan (oversimplified) for the patient is based on the above fundamental truth. One attempts to have the patient verbalize his anger and frustrations and "Get them out of him!"

AGGRESSIONS AND FRUSTRATIONS IN LOW KEY

The following three papers describe instances in which angers and frustrations are not verbalized but go underground with other kinds of resultant symptom formation suggestive of intense distress, and portray for the reader some of the "color" that may lead to suicide in certain instances.

Hippies and the Middle-Age Crisis

Essentially, the hippies are encouraged to express the discontents of their middle-aged parents, who are too fearful to acknowledge to themselves, let alone to someone else, the bleakness, rutlike existence and emptied idealism of their lives. For after all, where could such young people have experienced enough living to account for the faded and jaded appearances of their lives—the cynicism, discouragement, and sense of being ancient—unless they have by osmosis allowed themselves to adopt their parents' discontents and have mixed them into their protests?

The crisis of middle age, no matter when it happens chronologically (thirties, forties, fifties), is the revelation that "I have but one life and where is it going? It'll be a long time that I rot in the grave—and alone!" The sudden awareness that the routines of life have been so entrenched that the living that was supposed to be sustained by necessary routines has been submerged, squashed, and all but eliminated by the hypertrophy of these "means" is part of the revelation. The "crisis": "Where has it gone? Not so much my youth. But the idealism and love that seemed to flow in me?" So we have had our "flower children" who give us another chance at living rather than existing. But the tragedy is that they become only caricatures of that which we would want. Why? Because they embody everything that we are simultaneously. To the degree they fulfill our wishes, the "flower principle" stands out in the avowed purpose of love and idealism they possess. To the degree they embody our disillusionment with ourselves, they appear discontented, discouraged, inept, hopeless, and more ancient than the oldest of us. Hippies are a hysterical symptom of "middle-age crisis": the contained wishes, the defenses against their fruition, and the utter despair that it is the best we can do. How does a youth, being aware of his deadened parent, express life? It would be like flaunting it before the "aged one." "Look at what I can do, and you are dead!" What gross insensitivity! So the poor hippy often goes around when all is said and done, deadened like his parent. And, as we could surmise, this parent may not only be experiencing "middle-age crisis" but may also be in the throes of potential suicide crisis.

Hippies and Dream Robbers

Researchers have in recent years explored sleep and dreaming quite extensively. A great fund of basic fact has accumulated, and soon numerous connections to clinical phenomena will be established on sound ground. In the meantime, to share a speculation with the reader is very tempting.

The speculation centers upon some of the observations made about sleep and dream deprivation, especially the latter. As I understand it, if subjects are interrupted in their dreaming (rapid eye movement [REM] sleep, as detected by brain-wave examinations during sleep) although allowed to sleep at other stages (when not dreaming), a psychosis can be produced after a period of time. Conclusions have been subsequently offered that dreaming is essential to normal functioning. If poetic license is granted and we can equate dreaming with our wishes, aspirations, desires, hopes, instead of limiting the definition of dreaming to the strictly physiological processes measured by REM, I propose to speculate on dream deprivation manifested by the victims of nonexperimental dream robbers—the hippies and their drugs. Briefly, my premise is this: hallucinogenic drugs are used by the victim of dream robbing in order to restore and or preserve dreams that the parent or society cannot touch. To elaborate, the parents of moderately well-to-do drug users have often been very indulgent. Indeed, they have often attempted to provide material things for their offspring even before the latter can verbalize the desire for them. Rather than the child or youth being given the time to long for a car, it may be presented to him before he has even dreamed of having one. Facetiously, one might say that the parent in competition with the Joneses must demonstrate his acuteness in discovering the possible wishes or dreams of his child and show the world his ability to respond before his neighbor Jones does. That the provision of these items takes place during the earlier development years is understood. That there is a social counterpart to this seems most probable. For example, the possible fantasies a child might have had in the past are often depicted on the television set. A generation ago, the child had only the radio to supplement his reading. Visual imagery could still be his! His own imagination could produce some unique results. Certain dreams could still be his. But then consider how this area of life is disturbed by the provision of TV: exciting, stimulating visual imagery. It's all provided. Finally the protest comes out: "Leave me alone! I want to be by myself! Leave me to my own dreams!" And the parent responds: "What can I do for you?" "Get lost!" is the answer. But the parent dutifully persists. The alternative? The youth says: "If I must be subjected to their dream robbing, I'll have dreams that they couldn't possibly anticipate! They'll be so wild that they could never in 100 years come close to taking them from me.'' No longer able to dream his dream through natural means, he is literally forced by his dream robbers to elude to them with whatever hallucinogen is available. "I just need to be turned on." Even the phrase "turned on" has its tragic connotation in that it is the identical phrase that formerly would have been used to operate a stimulus-providing machine: one *turns on* a radio or television set. In other words, such a hippy-drug user has essentially identified himself with a machine, implying that he himself is not capable of imagination. Even the dreams he does provide for himself with his various drugs, he cannot claim credit for: "My drug gave it to me—they didn't take my dream away!''

The speculation above is not really so novel. Child therapists for years have discussed the necessity for parents to at times frustrate their children, rather than give them their every wish in order that the children could grow up. However, I'm not sure that the dream robbing has been as frequently emphasized. The human needs his dreams, his aspirations, and needs the opportunity to work for their realization. His curiosity, a native attribute, may be his tool for such realization. One sometimes wonders how some parents may be so blind to this curiosity in their children or why, rather than encouraging its development, they must squash it instead. It is almost as if they are afraid of being alive and curious, too. What will they see in themselves if they really look? It is almost as if children in their attempts to be alive remind their parents in too stark a fashion of what they, the parents, have already surrendered. It's too painful to be so reminded! And so they, the parents, are often only too relieved when their own children begin to show the signs of aging: dulled curiosity, conformity to the establishment in its most negative connotations. If one's own dreams have somehow been lost, one attempts to "rob" another, even one's own child. And now it is the child's turn to be a potential suicide crisis in contrast to the parent, as in the first paper.

Losing to Children — A Developmental Necessity

During the last several years, the subject of child abuse has received attention from everyone. With this stimulus, the author has had second thoughts about a young boy seen years ago and wonders whether the presenting symptoms—unhappiness, rarely playing with friends unless much younger, reluctance to attend school, fears of injury, and insomnia—had been manifestations of a special nuance of child abuse.

A description of a game in which the therapist could bring about the winning or losing with the patient highlights the therapy. Animal observations are used to support the hypothesis that the parent must indulge the growing small child's winning of games as a crucial aspect of development. Where the parent, out of his own exaggerated needs to win, be perfect, and so on, is not able to respond and lose to the youngster, a form of child abuse is in the making.

Currently, great attention is given to the problems of child abuse, with both the public and professionals increasingly aware not only of the obvious instances of trouble but also of the more subtle ramifications to which children might be subjected.

This spirit of the day may well have contributed to my reformulating thoughts about a seven-year-old boy I'll call Bill, seen years ago. Bill's parents described symptoms most pediatricians have heard from time to time: He was unhappy, even depressed; rarely played with friends, unless they were significantly younger than he; seemed very reluctant to attend school; was chronically concerned about getting injured should he fall or slip; and had sleeping difficulties that contributed to his irritability and wan appearance. His parents were college educated, sophisticated, and most desirous of extending efforts for their son, who they feared would become progressively handicapped should they delay initiating professional guidance.

On first meeting Bill, I found him to be rather restricted in his movements, very much on guard, but bravely consenting to leave his mother in the waiting room as we entered the "inner sanctum." I had suggested to Bill's parents that they tell him he was to be seeing a "talking" doctor rather than one who gives shots. Apparently that explanation, his wish to please his parents, plus his own native residual curiosity allowed him to overcome his inclination to be fearful in such a new situation. So we began. However, with youngsters this age, it can be very difficult to have them sit an entire session and focus on their problems as one might expect an adult to do. Besides, with this little fellow who was so much on guard, speaking eyeball to eyeball for more than a few minutes was beyond therapeutic expectations.

Often as a means of solving the above type of procedural dilemma, the therapist utilizes play activity as a means of seemingly diverting the youngster-patient and, in this more tangential fashion, elicit further information and conduct therapy. However, as mentioned earlier, Bill was too fearful to play the ordinary games or to color and draw, because, as it turned out, he was so concerned that he must be perfect. To be perfect, all the games had to be won and drawings had to be of the calibre of Leonardo's. We indeed had a dilemma. Fortunately, a card game evolved that we subsequently called "Flip." A deck of playing cards was divided, and one player proceeded to throw a card to the floor. The other player then attempted to cover some portion of the card with one he would throw. This would go on alternately, until one player succeeded and acquired all the previously thrown cards except for one—and the play would begin again. Each time a card was thrown, the word *Flip* was said. Winning and losing could easily be controlled by the therapist. As the reader can imagine, Bill won—and won, and won! For weeks, this was almost our only activity. Upon entering the consultation room, Bill would immediately exclaim, "Okay! Get the cards!"

Some variations were gradually perceptible. Rather than flipping the cards in a relatively confined area on the floor, Bill could gradually flip with greater abandon. In fact, he could get out of his chair and take other more advantageous positions in the room. A number of months later, we found ourselves able to graduate to other games of a more conventional nature, during which time I would again primarily lose and, often in crocodile tears, say to Bill, "Have you ever seen a grown psychiatrist cry?" "Yeah! You are funny!" he might respond, conceptualizing my message quite clearly and finding himself able to be beaten by me on occasion without undue upset.

Meanwhile, the parents would reassure me of Bill's progress. He was being successful elsewhere. Results were happening! He appeared more buoyant at home. Teachers described his being more at ease with his peers, more willing to engage in their games, and not as cramped in school assignments. Throughout the treatment, many discussions with the parents in the early months centered on "Flip" and why the game was being used. The necessity, as I saw it, of being able to allow Bill to win was crucial. And this was emphasized again and again to the parents who seemed to understand.

In spite of this emphasis and apparent comprehension by the parents, an episode occurred which clearly demonstrates the issue. Bill's family had gone away for a weekend to a university summer camp where Bill was taught chess by one of the other adults who apparently had the young boy enthused. The parents had also played chess in the past, and the boy desired to try out his new-found accomplishment with them. Mother subsequently called me just prior to Bill's next appointment to frantically explain how something horrible had happened and wanted me to be prepared. The previous evening she had played chess with Bill and she pathetically declared to me, "I accidentally beat him, because I don't know how to play the game well enough to lose!"

To me this experience epitomized the situation. Although bright, well educated, and now schooled about "Flip," mother's need to win and be successful won out. We can only wonder how often Bill had had comparable experiences. His father, too, was a driving, high-principled individual, with marked needs to win. That the parental needs could be so strong and inadvertently harm Bill was a ghastly paradox. For in their desire to win and be successful, they were equally desirous of being successful parents, and Bill's difficulties were being experienced as something not perfect in them!

Once when I presented this case to a general medical audience, one of the internists commented: "But, Irv, to lose to a child is unrealistic. That's not how the world is! When I play basketball with my kids, I play hard. If they get too close, I might give them an elbow! We play tough. That's life." At the time my colleague raised his objection I replied that, to my way of thinking, the child to whom the parent loses would not really have a distortion of his world. Even the very young child, recognizing the superior strength and knowledge of the adult, knows he has not really won the game. There is a form of tacit understanding that he has been allowed to win; to flex his muscles or brain cells and not be smashed by the parent for his presumptuousness!

Certain natural animal experiments have been observed

by me, the documentation of which I feel adds a sense of validity to my hypothesis. Until a year ago, we had one dog, a 75-pound, six-year-old male collie. At that time, we obtained an eight-pound, six-week-old male Australian shepherd and, within a week, they had developed a game of "tug o' war" using an old sock. Understandably, the collie could drag the puppy around at will. And this would be done a few times, though gently. More surprisingly and more frequently, it was the eight-pound puppy who pulled the collie around the room, growling and being as vicious as his little body would allow. The game was not quite "Flip," but the parallels were obvious. Even more remarkable were the second series of experiments, when several months later a young couple brought over their new male puppy, an Australian shepherd about six weeks old. Our puppy, now a grown adolescent of four to five months old and 25-30 pounds, compared to the seven-to-eight pound visitor, proceeded to reverse roles. The puppy visitor would pull him around, bark at him, and so on, as our puppy had so recently done with our older dog. And, when the puppy visitor left, our puppy returned to his role of aggressively pulling the collie around.

Akin to these more recent animal observations were those of years ago. A small, male Pomeranian-Spitz would tolerate my crawling infant son's pulling and punching him until when tired he would escape by hiding under a table. However, should one of the older children treat the dog similarly, no such patient indulgence would be forthcoming. Instead, some barking and even a warning bite would ensue. The dog's actions would seem to imply there is an age where indulgence of a child's active exploration of the world might include even suffered inconveniences by the parent-dog such as pulled hair and swatted nose. But once through this age, the more grown child should know better! Incidentally, it was not just my youngest child who could be indulged by the dog; the equally small infants of visitors would be treated similarly and not abused.

In summary, I am suggesting that the ability of the parent to indulge his growing small child in the winning of games is a crucial aspect of developmental experience where budding confidence, a natural outgrowth of a child's innate curiosity, has opportunities to flower and ripen. Where the parent, out of his own exaggerated needs to win, to be successful, or to be perfect, is not able to respond and play "Flip" games with his child, a form of child abuse is in the making. Crippled, even if he should reach the age of parenthood himself, such a child-parent would tend to repeat this unfortunate cycle. Child abuse, I suggest, may come in all sorts of forms.

AGGRESSION OF WOULD-BE RESCUER

In the preceding three papers, some of the interconnecting possibilities of victim and rescuer can be seen between the lines. These possibilities are more subtle than the gross presentation of my battered patient and her mother. However, the process of identification is relevant throughout. The internalized aggression of the victim has its potential counterpart in the aggression of the proposed rescuer. This theme has been stressed at various points in the preceding material. The ability to be "Johnnie on the spot" has to vary from individual (rescuer) to individual and from time to time. These human limitations, when contrasted to the potential suicide victim's demands, sometimes as restitution for previous privations experienced, can readily create the possible explosiveness of crisis. When the rescuer's threshold is reached, a response like "Kill yourself, already! I'll give you the gun!" has not been infrequent, as already indicated by certain earlier examples. The more usual experience of guilt in the survivor often reflects this feeling but in an attenuated form: "What else could I have done? Did I show too much impatience; could I have been kinder?'' Other concerns of the potential rescuer relate to what we might call his culturally endowed ambivalence for the role: ''Is it polite to be nosey? How do you ask someone if he or she is going to commit suicide? What right do I have to enter the privacy of another?'' Some of these feelings are so ingrained that to assume the role of rescuer could be tantamount to defying one of the Ten Commandments! The would-be rescuer, when he misses his cue, may be inadvertently contributing to the suicide. For the chosen rescuer, too, may have had his own problems with which to deal, not being ready for his designated role. To recognize the role also requires the heavy responsibility of acceptance. When other responsibilities weigh heavily upon the potential rescuer, additional weights may be avoided. In the process, the rescue message is not seen or acted upon. This in itself can be unbearable for the survivor, who may well need to be protected should ''his victim'' fatally pursue his course of action. Even when we know that others, too, have missed their role as rescuer, we can be beside ourselves with grief and guilt.

The mental gyrations that ensue to deal with guilt are legion. A short story may give us some comic relief: The youngster was being told the facts of life by a rather dramatic parent. ''Look, Johnnie. You must not have intercourse with a little girl. You must not. You must not get on *top* of a little girl. For, if you do, you will *kill* her!'' With those thoughts on his mind, little Johnnie on the Spot went to bed for a good night's sleep. The following day, as luck would have it, he met Tillie, his precocious neighbor. ''Hey, Johnnie! Let's *screw!*'' Protesting, Johnnie explained what he had been told the previous night—especially that he should never get on *top* of a girl! ''Oh, Johnnie. It'll be alright! *I'll get on top.*'' Having cut through his reticence with superb counterargument, Tillie was on top when she swooned in ecstacy, collapsing beside our hero, Johnnie. Thinking that his parent's warnings had come true, he jumped to his feet and started running, "Oh, my God! I've killed her!" Suddenly he stopped in his tracks. "Hey! *I didn't kill her. She committed suicide!"* Such a story seems a bit bizarre but obviously points out how gross fantasies may be, how one can be so preoccupied with one's own needs to the exclusion of the other's, and the tragicomic results that can evolve. Just to remind the reader of more practical scenes (or relevant) to the above story: the suicide attempt or completed suicide of a young girl that might have related to her finding out that she was pregnant. Not knowing how to handle such a crisis, and being overwhelmed, no alternative seemed available.

Whenever I use an example of the youngster who may have hysterical dramatic features, I realize that I run the risk of conveying possible erroneous conclusions to the reader: that I am either not taking my subject of suicide seriously or that the subject itself is not serious or that the ideas themselves are not worthy of consideration. Hopefully, the reader will not draw such conclusions. The tortured feelings both of the suicidal person and of the would-be rescuer are all too clear. The young girl who literally chews on her wrists in angry bites is symbolically and (in her psychosis) actually killing *the other* contained in her body. This gross sight (again, a true experience witnessed years ago in a hospital setting) teaches us what may at other times take place only symbolically in the suicidal person met in other settings and at other times. Science has often learned through exaggerated cases, where motifs are stark and nonambiguous, what may go on in the less exaggerated cases. More importantly for our specific discussion, the lay person reads innuendos of anger and sees it sometimes in a subliminal fashion, I grant, but very accurately. In summary, the suicide person does convey his anger (as well as his wish to be rescued) to his would-be rescuer. And it is to be understood that the proposed rescuer may register accurately just this type of anger (rather than the wish to be rescued) and respond accordingly—and obviously not to the benefit of the potential victim. In such cases, the rescuer allows the suicide to happen or attempts to "dump" the problem. Even if the rescuer is able to control his anger, on a chronic basis, his energies get depleted.

However, it may be helpful to the rescuer to reemphasize to himself or herself that *some* of the anger of the suicide person is related to his or her more central core of anxiety at the thought that no person or thing can really help. Nothing will avail. Mr. Z dramatically illustrated this point with his crustiness and seeming obnoxiousness. As family and physicians were progressively being worn out, Mr. Z's crescendo of complaints would intensify the wearing out process in his would-be rescuers. His underlying depression and suicidal potential were being masked in the process and becoming more and more critical as he interpreted the reactions of those about him as convincing proof that no one cared. A self-fulfilling prophecy would have finally contributed to his suicide.

Knowing that other suicidal persons may operate in a similar fashion—or sometimes be more subtle—may help the rescuer cut through to the heart of the matter rather than being put off and becoming just another of the victim's rejectors. It's striking and bears repeating that we, as rescuers, have our feelings too! Not comprehending how a Mr. Z might function, we easily perceive his attitudes as rejecting us! Among other points, the following material contains the exaggeration of this phenomenon.

EXPRESSING THE AGGRESSION: STAGES OF RECOVERY

On contemplating the classic understanding of the dynamics of suicide—that is, anger turned in on oneself—a set of clinical observations comes to mind that brings additional conviction to the aptness of this theoretical position. In addition, certain practical offshoots may appear better outlined for the rescuer who is to be given another chance. What I have in mind is the following.

Given the circumstances of a person overdosing, coming to the verge of death, being maintained by an artificial respiratory machine, and, fortunately, surviving, I have observed a sequence of expressed emotion as the person returns in the direction of life that I believe mirrors the original sequence (in reverse direction) towards death.

Although Mr. X (the man whom I described earlier) hung himself rather than overdosed, we can recall from his writings the back and forth wishes for life he experienced in the several days before his death. Also, we can recall his asking for forgiveness for what he was about to do. Likewise, his anger and rage impressed us. But he dies. And so we do not have immediate reactions should he have lived. In contrast, the person I have in mind with Figure 6.1 lived. Had there been written notes before ingestion of pills, I would imagine they would have been very similar to Mr. X's or to notes left by others who have died by overdosing. Mixtures of repentance and rage are frequently cited in the literature. What I feel has been underemphasized is the immediate period of recovery containing the rage, repentance, and anger. It is like observing an individual coming out of an anesthetic (the parallels physiologically are identical), where the primitiveness of the emotions is displayed. This is an extraordinarily dangerous group of phases for the rescuer-suicide person "system." Pitfalls abound for the rescuer at several distinct points during the process of recovery.

First, it would concern me should rescuers (relatives, friends, or physicians) find themselves reacting to the "coming out" rage (they don't ordinarily see the "going in" rage) of the victim: "Get the hell out of here! You fucking bastards leave me die!" These are not exact quotations, but they convey the spirit. The grotesque rage in its primitiveness has frequently turned a potential rescuer back. "How can he say things like that to me, to the children? If he hates us so, perhaps he should die!" The paradox is that the rescuer, who may have not quite recognized his or her role the first time around, may once again be unavailable, having recoiled with disbelief and horror from such rage issuing forth from the loved one. The victim may have been depressed, yes; but not filled with such hate! The latter emotion (and directed at the rescuer) is surprising—so full of hurt, to say the least.

Second, is the "coming out" phase of repentance. Here, the victim may beg forgiveness, may go on to say, "I didn't mean it. It was only an accident. I was drinking too much and wasn't able to really keep count of the pills. . . I just needed to sleep a little. I'm so sorry I frightened you and caused such worry. I would never do it again." The danger is that the rescuer is lulled into thinking that perhaps it was all "just an accident." Besides, after the previous rage, this phase is such a relief. Rescuers want to be loved, too! And, once again the rescuer may wish to blot out the responsibility of his rescue function, feeling that everyone has just overreacted! All's now well with the world.

Third in the sequence of recovery is the phase of anger. At this point, the suicidal person having gone through the repenting phase may again upset his potential rescuer. No longer raging, he nevertheless is angry and harangues. "It's no use. I should really have died. You don't really care. Things aren't really going to be changed. Why did you side with the kids when I was trying to discipline them? You're always undercutting me." Understandably, having blame heaped on one does not bring out the best in the would-be rescuer at this phase either.

When I used the word *recovery,* I did not want the reader to be inadvertently misled. I am using the word to refer to the psychological state to which the suicide person may hopefully attain *after* (maybe many months later!) he or she is stabilized and has recovered from the physical ordeal. Again, the rescuer should not confuse the two types of recovery—physical and psychological—even when the physician says, "He's OK now!" This is not true. For after physical recovery and the three phases described immediately above, the patient has only reached the *depression* stage from which he plunged into the overdose in the first place. To avert a second suicide attempt, the rescuer has to feel that certain constuctive processes have been initated that could lead to recovery in the psychological sense. One would hope that the follow-through would be successful. (See Chapter 9 for additional discussion of follow-through rescue problems).

The "J'accuse!" attitude—the rage—is not present in all suicides, but its presence in many, I believe, requires underscoring, even when it is not seemingly directed at a given person. As mentioned with the CUSS patients, the Fates can be blamed with comparable vehemence. However, from a rescuer's point of view, the phenomenon requires the personal awareness of being on guard to preserve one's rescuer functioning when attacked. It is very difficult not to feel pushed away when challenged or accused by the victim. To remain steadfast when the victim is implying (or stating directly) "How dare you be happy when I'm so miserable!" takes great stamina and love.

Chapter 7

SOCIETY'S REACTIONS TO SUICIDES OR WOULD-BE SUICIDES

Outright Anger at the Suicide

Against the Law. For centuries legal sanctions have existed against the suicidal person. Perhaps this represents a more global societal response paralleling the more individual personal rescuer reaction described at the conclusion of the previous chapter. Indeed, as recently as the last century, certain societies might actually have hanged the suicidal person who had survived his own self-destructive act. If the suicide person should live, he could be placed in jail according to the letter of the law. In my personal experience, I don't know of a single such incarceration. But I do not know for a fact that it has not taken place. About 20 years ago, in an acute psychiatric hospital setting, what I do clearly remember is the routine fact of policemen (usually in pairs) being required to question the suicide survivor and make a written police report. The embarrassment and added sense of indignity were perhaps to be society's warning to the survivor not to do it again! That society has recognized intuitively some of the dynamics of the suicide person (e.g., his desire to kill the other) seems most likely to explain what otherwise would seem to be an incomprehensible law.

ANTIRELIGIOUS. Certain religious groups have likewise recognized the aggression in the suicidal person and for centuries expressed their disfavor toward the suicide by refusing him burial in hallowed ground. Other religious services might also be omitted—to the further grief of the survivors, one would think. On the other hand, is it possible to conceptualize the practice as a further way to remove guilt from the rescuer and to place it on the suicide victim where, since he is dead, it won't hurt anyway? One wonders. Over and beyond our speculations, we do know that the suicidal person has challenged our belief in a better world tomorrow (heaven) by his act. He obviously does *not* believe in this better world. He is downright unreligious! So it is no wonder that he has had the wrath of God placed on his head by religious groups —especially in the past.

"STOP! YOU'RE MAKING ME DEPRESSED!" The suicidal person is a reminder of our own potential for depression or our own loss of idealism. This may help explain or give some rationale for the poor insight of some otherwise highly intelligent people who might have been better rescuers. Depression, even of an attenuated form, is warded off by whatever means possible. When another person speaks of his miserable situation, it cannot but frequently stir areas of comparison in the listener. And this can be just too much! "Better that I don't hear you; then I don't have to hear myself!" In some situations, the anger at the suicidal person for disturbing our equilibrium shows itself in sarcasm and depreciation. Even physicians may sometimes screen from their own consciousness the awareness that a patient who is presenting himself with numerous physical symptoms is experiencing some depression—perhaps a great deal. Again, to recognize depression (even when it might not have reached suicidal proportions) in any one person results in the recognition of our own capacity to be depressed.

LIBERAL VIEWPOINT

Perhaps as a response to society's anger at the suicidal person, as exemplified by some of the above, others, originally out of empathy for the suicidal person, have taken a rather extreme position—namely, that the suicidal person has the *right* to suicide. From a philosophical stance, they raise the question of whether individual freedom is being violated by placing prohibitions on suicide or even trying to curtail it. Some proponents of the liberal position cite instances of severe debilitating illness to further support their view that suicide (or euthanasia) be practiced. Indeed, some of their arguments have convincing tones. However, my impression is that their position (with exaggerated cases that represent a minute number of the actual cases of suicide) tends to blind us in our role of resucer where we really could perform a useful function, where the suicidal person would want us to perform as rescuer. Even where such a liberal may find an example that he believes supports his view, he may cloud the issue. For example, a writer on one of our popular news magazines beautifully portrayed his own personal experiences with severe illness only to conclude that some of the patients dying with their diseases should be released from their misery by suicide. That he himself was almost as seriously ill and possibly in a similar state of mind was "forgotten"—a mechanism probably common to those of us who survive "by almost a miracle." From such a vantage point, that of surviving, he would inadvertently preclude the possibility of recovery for some other individuals of this group by too readily advocating the means of their demise.

Understandably, his writing was in good faith. There are times with certain patients that one wonders whether one is functioning as a healer-rescuer or as a type of demon, sadistically keeping alive a "vegetable" with our intravenous fluids, heart-lung machines, and the like. Ordinarily, the trained physician knows which role he is serving. The layman, even though intelligent, may not for sure be able to distinguish these roles as he observes various tubes and machinery hooked up to his neighboring patients. And if he himself has a cloudy sensorium due to illness and or drugs administered, his judgment about these roles of rescuer or devil may be detrimentally affected. Likewise, his ability to distinguish the wish to live from the wish to die in his bedside companions may be equally diminished. The rationale that an expert newsman who is superb in his abilities to judge political events is likewise equally adept at making medical judgments is about as logical as assuming that a psychiatrist supposedly expert in dealing with emotions is equally qualified to make political pronouncements! That experts in one field often go about acting as if they are experts in all others is a common enough phenomenon. That its frequency makes it a legitimate activity is another matter! The political scientist or psychiatrist who does so deserves our criticism no matter how fine his intentions.

However, I do not want to leave this short section on the liberal viewpoint without better acknowledging some of the serious questions that might be raised. Following a lecture on suicide, a member of the audience asked regarding the rescuer's role in the following situation: "How can you help a person who has been left partially disabled by a stroke? The patient has partial speech, loss of use of right arm, and gets very depressed at times. He is 62 years old and has been this way for three years. He has continued to take acupuncture treatments weekly for the past year, but they do not seem to be helping." Our empathy and sympathy go out to such a person and his rescuers. The person and his family have been apparently willing to try whatever means that might promise cure—including acupuncture. Yet, I wonder at their fully comprehending and accepting the neurological limitations of the man's brain injury. In contrast to other tissues of the human body that may make excellent recoveries subsequent to injury, the brain tissue is very limited in recovery. Does the patient and the family know this? If they do not, persistence of unrealizable hopes gives rise to further aggravation and irritations. The patient-victim may feel his family thinks of him as a shirker—one who is not trying hard enough to recover. On the other hand, he might feel the family is not really all that concerned or obtaining the right consultants or medication. Again, members of the family can have the same set of questions from their vantage point. What is necessary is a therapist who can strongly assert the facts and limitations to both patient and family, so that appropriate acceptance and mourning of lost functions might take place. Additional physiotherapy including some retraining might aid in a partial fashion. The basic principles center on the fact that certain functions that have customarily been circuited through now damaged pathways in the brain may be accomplished by establishing new circuits traversing undamaged brain tissue. Certain respected medical centers, often university connected, have departments devoted to just this form of retraining. Likewise, their personnel can be extremely realistic about limitations. Families of stroke victims need to know that, even where speech involvement is extensive, the victim may understand very well what is said. He or she is not a "vegetable." Comprehending accurately the limitations and residual assets of the victim does not magically remove the severe problems. But at least it does not further burden either victim or family member with unrealistic expectations and demands, which in turn contributes to an accentuation of depression and mutual disrespect.

INVOLVED VERSUS NONINVOLVED

Supposedly, the Oriental idea is that once you have acted in the role of rescuer and saved, you owe the person saved—you must maintain him. If you interfere with a man's right to die (or save him when he might want to be saved), you've got to make it worthwhile. Life is to be better. In spirit, this would be a specific cultural recognition of the psychological principle I mentioned and stressed in the case immediately following Mr. X's journal. Once the role of rescuer is initiated, the follow-through must be energetically continued with unabated enthusiasm lest the suicide person construe waning or partially suspended rescue efforts as the ultimate rejection. The difficulty of providing proper, effective, and continual follow-up to the suicide person is enormous. The energies required may be astronomical. Rather than criticizing those agencies or people dedicated to providing these services, thereby reducing their energies by putting them on the defensive, society at large might do well to mobilize certain liberals in the pursuit of other areas of social concern.

OUTRIGHT ANGER AT PSYCHIATRISTS, CLINICS, AND OTHER FAILED RESCUERS

The anger at the rescuer who fails in his role is tremendous. In my opinion, it is this anger that gives rise to so many psychiatry jokes and, at times, lies beneath some of the "liberal" pronouncements. Not only is the suicide person to be given the right to suicide, but trying to give him psychiatric help in the first place is really a waste of time. It won't really help. Consider the following frequently heard barb: "Anyone who sees a psychiatrist, must *really* need his head examined!" Or the definition of psychiatry: "The study of the id by the odd!'' Several additional considerations may be mentioned regarding anger at the psychiatrists and clinics who fail to save.

There is an understandable human desire to lodge power in the therapist and a consequent disappointment (to say the least) if suicide does happen. The sense of disappointment is often in proportion to the magic originally invested. Society has always had its rescuers, ever since our original models—the first parents. Certain surrogate parents were designated either by specific skills possessed or expressed desire to become the rescuers (healers) of the particular society. The medicine men of certain cultures (witch doctors, religious shamans) were predecessors of our doctors, clergy, psychiatrists today. In their way, they may have had some positive effect. Otherwise, their roles with modifications would not have continued from culture to culture. But the aura of magic persists. Society may influence today's professional rescuers to utilize certain forms of magic in the care of their ill, including suicidal persons. If the essential needs are being met, a little magic won't hurt. Specifically, I would deplore the use of medication with the suicidal person if the underlying motifs of depression and anger were not being simultaneously discussed. Otherwise, the therapist is acting out *his* belief in magic by just prescribing pills! Magic frequently relates to the patient–physician (therapist) relationship. All that is necessary is the proper pushing of buttons or swallowing of pills, and the suicide person will be relieved of his depression! If not quite that fast, his relief of perhaps long-standing problems should come as quickly as someone recovering from a cold (seven days or one week, as the joke goes); maybe a little longer—like someone recovering from a broken arm (six weeks, perhaps). That certain areas of neurosis may have existed for years and are difficult to modify is almost an impossible concept to accept. Certain individuals have acquired emotional scars that defy altering. Diabetics may need insulin the rest of their lives.

Yet, their doctors are not vilified for their continued treatment. Some psychiatric problems of select individuals might be seen in the same context. And the psychiatrists treating such individuals are no more to be condemned than the physicians treating the diabetic who may have his death from insulin reactions or diabetic coma.

Fortunately, the usual suicide person is one who has more resilience than those immediately listed above. Their therapies prove by and large quite helpful. Incidentally, the impatience society may have toward the psychiatrists is more than matched by the impatience relatives may have toward certain depressed, suicidal persons. A woman, separated four months from her husband, related some of these feelings: "My parents are saying that I should forget the *bastard!* They tell me that there are a lot of other fish in the sea, and wonder when I'll finally get over him! If I'm with them for a few hours and I smile or laugh, they think I'm perfectly well. A day or two later when I'm down again they ask, 'What's happening to you now?' They seem so bewildered and can't seem to comprehend that I remain basically miserable even though I have my moments of light-heartedness. And they're so goddamned critical, making me feel like an imbecile for still being depressed!" We can readily empathize with the patient, seeing clearly how she feels misunderstood by her relatives. Not forgetting that being misunderstood is somewhat equivalent to being rejected, we remain very concerned for her. On the other hand, one can empathize with parents and relatives who feel helpless toward the woman; they cannot bring her husband back. As the sensation of helplessness increases, they try to get rid of it. And one of the ways is to play ostrich—pretend that the woman is *not* so depressed. Certainly she should not remain depressed. "The nerve of her! Can't she realize..." At times the therapist can get this idea across to the patient and relieve this area of concern, giving the patient a better chance of preserving these relationships when she better comprehends that the relatives' sense of helplessness relates to their real love for her and their own impotence at the sight of her distress.

Another consideration in regard to anger at therapists lies in the acknowledged characteristic that certain therapists possess—namely, their own sense of omnipotence, which may contribute to a less than real approach to their patients or clients. "I, myself, will save you!" minimizing the real intensity of feeling in the patient. The role of rescuer (whether performed by psychiatrist, clergy, or lay individual) has its appeal in terms of the stereotyped glories that go with one serving such a function. To feel so important in the lives of others is an attractive inducement for many. That *some* of this feeling should accrue the efforts of the rescuer seems only just payment. However, if the grandiose motif is too much with the rescuer, he ultimately fails the persons who seek him out. Magic, whether in the mind of the suicidal person or his rescuer, is not the proper medicine! Of course, other blind spots occur in therapists besides that of omnipotence. It is just that omnipotence is one of the most glaring. To be aware of our blind spots is crucial to the conduct of any therapy. Understandably, the inability to look at our own depressive potential is the epitome of blind spots when working with the suicidal person.

A third factor contributing to anger at therapists is the guilt of the rescuer or survivor. Whenever guilt plagues an individual, anyone or anything that will remove it is utilized. It is a most horrible feeling tone, as already acknowledged. So, the therapist often can be the convenient place to displace these ill feelings. "It's the therapist's fault." Interestingly, this complaint is infrequently lodged, however. To give most rescuer survivors credit, they do not so quickly place their burdens upon the therapist—at least not directly. Indirect newspaper accounts or magazine articles may indicate anger or disrespect. But for the most part the rescuer survivor wants to put the matter to rest. One particular personal experience that was an exception took place many years ago during a discussion subsequent to my presenting an abbreviated version of this book's theme to a general medical audience. One of the doctors, who had previously been most friendly toward me and had indicated his awareness of psychiatric issues on numerous previous occasions, spoke up with what I felt was extraordinary anger and feeling against my lecture. He had felt that I had treated the matter lightly (especially with the series of cartoons regarding clues to suicide). And his criticisms were repeated in several different ways to the extent I was made to feel most uncomfortable, to say the least. Finally, at the end of his diatribe, he went on to explain to the audience the reason for his fury with me—namely, that his brother had committed suicide while a college student many years earlier. He went on to further discuss the fact that the brother's suicide had been very unexpected in that he had received a letter from him only several days prior to the tragedy. Putting ourselves into the shoes of my former colleague, we could imagine the possibility of his feeling somewhere within himself sensations of having "missed the clue." My emphasizing the theme of rescuer must have felt like an accusing finger going right through him. The agony of it had to be displaced. Where better to put it than upon the person who was lecturing and inferring such evil things about possible rescuers? Lecturing (and even in a book where one has more space and opportunity for amplification) always has the risk of being too condensed. In the process, it is so easy to fail to make the full emphasis with clarifications and qualifications. Instead of comprehending the cartoons as pictorial examples of my theme, the materials suggested a mockery of the whole subject! In all fairness to my colleague, I had failed to emphasize again and again the seriousness of my presentation by not repeating preliminary warnings (as I did in my Foreward and throughout this book) that my use of humor was just a device to make a gruesome subject a bit more bearable.

Chapter 8

SENSE OF RESPONSIBILITY— WHERE DOES IT LIE?

Who is responsible? This is the basic question and one that is most uncomfortable. It is no wonder that there evolves a collusion of sorts in which many may unwittingly participate. Understandably, the purpose of this collusion is to be removed from responsibility the best one can. And this is quite human! Guilt is a most miserable feeling. If one cannot shed it completely, at least one can spread it around a little. Enclosed in this section is material derived from several cartoons observed through the years that embody some of the techniques that have evolved in this "spreading around." Let's enumerate. One depicts a child holding his mother's hand leaving a therapist's office saying to another child about to enter: "Watch out for this guy! Instead of blaming your mother, he'll try to make *you* responsible for your behavior!" Interestingly, the older the person seeing this cartoon, the more likely he is to respond with laughter.

PARENTS

When we are young, obviously we have to depend greatly on our parents who do have great influence on our development. And a young person seeing this cartoon does not think it to be too funny, for if you are still holding mother's hand (as in the cartoon) you are not "free," and the parents do have the control. However, growth toward adulthood has to be predicated on a letting go of the hand with a simultaneous increase of responsibility—a process that has many starts and stops. But the majority of us get there. However, this tendency to blame parents or early experiences is so common that it, in turn, has given rise to numerous misunderstandings regarding therapy. Most important is the feeling that the therapist does spend all his time in cahoots with the patient upbraiding parents. And any intelligent lay person intuitively realizes that such activity goes nowhere—if that's all there is to it. We have all had "miserable" parents—more or less. But what have *we* done with it? What are we doing with it right now? The importance of our "ancient" family histories and our explorations of them lies in uncovering tendencies we have to repeat the old themes in new settings and with new characters (spouses, bosses, and so on). To the degree that the old themes are pleasant, we do not have to analyze them. To paraphrase Freud: Don't analyze away a good thing! When the old themes are being replayed and are negative or miserable, that is where therapy has a lot to offer. It helps separate out that which belongs to the past and that which appropriately belongs to the present.

THERAPISTS

An interesting variation of the above "blame of parents" is the "blame of therapists." Essentially, the premise is that "I, the patient, have placed myself in your hands and what have you done for me? *You* haven't gotten me well. In fact, your own neurosis has complicated my life and has contributed to your not helping me." The accusations have an old ring that sounds only too familiar. If one would put the name *parent* in place of the word *therapist*, the themes would sound almost identical. "You, parents and therapists, have me in your power to shape me, bring me to health and joy, and because of your own crazy hangups cause me my troubles."

Admittedly, therapists may have their difficulties and areas of psychic distress. And these may, indeed, interfere with the best therapy. It does occur. However, the occurrence the patient must keep an eye open for is his own tendency to shift responsibility upon the therapist as he might have previously done with the parent or spouse. This tendency to shift responsibility can in some instances be quite subtle. A salesman came to consult and in his first meeting with me wanted my opinion as to whether he was lazy or neurotic. He revealed that he was a supersalesman who would begin working for an organization and within two or three months be acclaimed by the other workers and superiors as the one who would soon be the president of the organization. "I characteristically zoom to the top and then begin to fizzle. I no longer keep my appointments, take in movies during the day instead of seeing and developing customers, and in general begin to fail." After a series of such starts and failures, it was no wonder my patient was feeling the pressures of his family.

At first, my inclination was to answer his first question—"Am I lazy or neurotic?"—with the latter possibility. He must be neurotic. I should give him the benefit of the doubt, especially since he seemed willing to spend his hard-earned money on therapy. It was the least I should do. Yet, after several additional meetings with this man, it became apparent through various remarks that the reason for his initial question was the following: If he were *lazy*, his wife and family would be on his back and blame him for his difficulties. And he would become more and more depressed.

If he were *neurotic*, no one could blame him. He could get off the hook. He was doing his best. He was seeing a psychiatrist, and it was the psychiatrist's fault—the damned SOB just hadn't discovered the answer yet! When I was able to point out this underlying attitude to the patient, we were both able to laugh. He acknowledged that he had been living his life with just that kind of attitude. We were then able to get down to business and subsequently deal with the neurosis behind his behavior. Without clarification of where the responsibility lies, there would have been no treatment and no let up of his ultimate depression.

GENETICS, CHEMISTRY

Genetics and chemistry represent other foci upon which responsibility may be placed. Serious investigators still pursue research in these fields to discover why certain individuals commit suicide. The assumption is that there is some inborn error of metabolism or genetic disturbance that makes individuals more susceptible to life's strains and thus prone to suicide. That future investigations will uncover additional factors that affect our physical and mental beings is most likely. But even then, the proportion of suicides that occur for those discovered reasons would be representative of an extremely small number. The research should continue, but by no means should it camouflage for us the fact that the large majority of suicidal persons are built like us, talk like us, and "There for the Grace of God go we."

We respect the gains workers have obtained in clarifying functions of amino acids, enzymes and other physiological elements, but as a means of explaining suicide, to my mind this again represents a red herring. Various chemical imbalances might conceivably prove vital to a few select individuals, but again, a minute number, when all is said and done. For those individuals involved, such research is important. It will help clarify certain basic scientific questions but not really contribute to a better essential undertanding of suicide. An analogy from the field of surgery might help emphasize my point. For many years, it has been good general surgical practice to incise and drain abcesses. The fact that antibiotics came on the scene relatively late and may also be used to combat abcesses does not do away with the fundamental incision and drainage concept. The old piece of knowledge remains extremely useful today. Indeed, there are situations where the antibiotics are powerless—situations not readily accessible to these potent drugs yet where application of the old concept continues to provide relief. Similarly, our body chemistries may be better understood in the future, we may have mood elevators of the most sophisticated type and so on, but it will remain fundamental to understand the feelings, attitudes, and thoughts lying behind a person's depression before giving him or her drugs, or else we run the risk of our patient suiciding with a smile on his face. We've "corrected" his mood, but left the same miserable thoughts!

PSYCHOSIS

Psychosis has been another area upon which the responsibility of suicide has been placed. For some of the religious (and legal) groups this "cause" of suicide has been somewhat welcomed in that anger or recriminations at the suicidal person can be more or less attenuated or eliminated. The rationale that the person did not know what he or she was really doing makes it possible to bury these individuals in the regular fashion with no further onerous fanfare. The victims were not in their right mind and they did not know that they were offending religious or legal principles. One cannot punish them further. That the overwhelmed mind on occasion presents as a disjointed or a psychotic mind is true.

But not all psychotic individuals commit suicide (although underlying depression may well exist). More importantly for our discussion, not all suicides are psychotic; most suicides occur in people described by those who knew them as sane—like you and me. This may be frightening to have it presented this way, but, to my knowledge, this is the way it is. And for us to fool ourselves about this point, thinking that these desperate persons must be "crazy," would tend to blind us to the clues when they are being emitted by our friends or relatives—for after all, they are "normal" just like you and me! Only crazy people commit suicide, and so all we have to do is keep an eye open for the kooks among us. It just does not work that way.

GOD

What about God? Should the responsibility be placed on God? Some people will lodge the responsibility here, you know. "God's will," "The ways of the Lord are just not known to us mortals." Without debating whether God exists or not, I will say, and the more religious reader may agree with me, "God helps those who help themselves!" This motto would seem to be one accepted by most faiths. To my way of thinking, such a motto allows us to remain more alert and available as potential rescuers. Otherwise, leaving it all to God would be similar to putting our faith in genetics, chemistry, or what have you—we would actually be disavowing our responsibility as human beings to utilize what we actually possess right now if and when we are approached by the would-be suicidal person. As human beings (religious or otherwise) it behooves us to utilize ourselves to fullest advantage. If God, chemistry, genetics work on our side, so much the better. A story about the contrasting ways one might relate to God follows:

The very pious, orthodox one who sat in the synagogue three times a day praying year after year was one morning surprised to see Jake the Gambler come in after an absence of 20 years. Jake walked quickly to the front of the synagogue, looked up through the ceiling to the heavens, and said, "God, I've placed $500 to win on Traife, the longshot. Let the horse win!" With that, he turned on his heels and strode out only to return that evening. The eyes of the pious one watched him again address words to the heavens, "Thanks, God!" After which he disappeared. At this point, the pious one could no longer contain himself: "Why, God? Why? Here I am a *real* religious man these many years, praying to you at least three times a day, and my daughter has married poorly, my wife is in ill health, my partners are stealing me blind. And Jake the Gambler who hasn't prayed to you in years, you grant his wish. Why, God, Why?" Suddenly, lightening flashed, thunder rolled, and in a booming voice God answered: "I'll tell you why! You bother me too much!!" The point of the story has always remained with me, primarily because I know some of the storyteller's personal life experiences of survival from Nazi concentration camps. His *own* activity resulted in his managing to survive. He was his own rescuer—he helped himself. When his group was asked by his captors who could operate a particular kind of equipment, he quickly raised his hand (and learned on the job). The others who failed to raise their hands died. Jake was a different kind of gambler from the one portrayed earlier in this book who relied on Lady Luck or the Fickle Finger of Fate. We could bet our bottom dollar that Jake was the type of gambler who paid off the jockeys and prayed to God for good measure!

Parents, early life experiences, psychiatrists, genetics, chemistry, psychoses, and God—all can be implicated in our question: Sense of responsibility—Where does it lie? To simplify, once again consider the suicide person and his rescuer. We can be hardnosed like the psychiatrist in yet another cartoon, "There you go, evading responsibility again. What about my bill?", as his patient is ready to jump from his window. It is difficult to make this emphasis without appearing utterly heartless. The suicide person is responsible for his actions! Straight and simple. If he should die, he is responsible for his action. True. He is responsible for *all* his actions—those almost perceptible acts suggestive of his wish to be rescued, also. He is responsible for his rescue message's quality, ambiguity, urgency, whatever. Likewise, he is responsible for choice (select or diffuse) of his rescuer. But it is so easy to "slip it on to the rescuer"—Am I lazy or neurotic? Often magically, the suicide person hopes a rescuer will materialize. Yes, we as rescuers feel our responsibility. Hopefully, we will be on our toes at the appropriate times, picking up the clues indicative of the wish to be rescued after sifting through the "magic" cloaking the message. We do not exist in a vacuum, even the most schizophrenic of us. From the moment of our conception, we are with someone—perhaps setting the stage or model for our continued sense of wishing to be connected. That we, the rescuers, also have this need makes us the more able to empathize with the suicidal person, who even in his state of extreme disenchantment with his world may emit veiled messages directed toward the living whom he hopes will share the responsibility of his surviving. It seems fitting in this context to quote the poet John Donne:

> No man is an *Iland,* intire of it selfe; every man
> is a peece of the *Continent,* a part of the *maine;* if
> *Clod* bee washed away by the Sea, *Europe* is the lesse,
> as well as if a *Promontorie* were, as well as if a *Mannor*
> of thy *friends* or of *thine owne* were; any mans *death*
> diminishes *me,* because I am involved in *Mankinde;* And
> therefore never send to know for whom the *bell* tolls;
> It tolls for *thee.*

Chapter 9

SOME FOLLOW-THROUGH RESCUE PROBLEMS

The prime emphasis of this book has been the immediate recognition of the rescuer's role. All of us at one time or another may be provided messages, and the issue has been whether we would acknowledge and accept what we are presented. Factors describing both the obscurity of messages sent by the suicidal person and the refusal to see on the part of the rescuer have been repeated several times in one fashion or another. At this time, a few more words about the follow-through are required, even though this has not been the central focus of the book.

As you remember, certain examples of the rescue process have been given, such as my 7:30 AM caller, in which the process was initiated satisfactorily only to fail later when not enough follow-through was supplied. It is one thing for the rescuer to recognize his role. It is another thing for the suicidal person to be convinced the rescuer will really rescue! Examples of better follow-through with their complexities and problems, can be seen with these additional stories:

SUICIDE PERSON'S PRIDE

A woman called one Sunday, desperately concerned about her husband, whom she felt was in need of psychiatric help. Her married daughter was on a telephone extension and concurred about the necessity of help for her father. However, the man was refusing to come to the phone himself, let alone to set up an office appointment. "*You* go if you think something needs to be done!" he said to his wife. An appointment was arranged for the next day, with the hope that the husband, too, would change his mind and come, but he didn't. Instead, the wife arrived by herself and gave the following history. Her husband was a diabetic, requiring insulin medication, which in the past weeks he had refused to take. He was also telling his daughter that he was going to get his papers in order. The crescendoing of his depression, irritability, periods of crying seemed to have followed the discovery that his sibling was seriously ill and was expected to die soon. Rather than obvious mourning, the designated patient demonstrated to his family excessive anger, at times confusion, and a general withdrawal and distancing, making it next to impossible for the family to approach him. They were beside themselves. Having recognized and acknowledged his suicide potential, what were they to do?

Let's first analyze together some of the things actually done. His spouse *did* come in for an appointment. She was told that most likely she *was* right—namely, that her husband could well be mourning the anticipated death of his sibling in spite of his seeming belligerence. When one cannot express hate and anger with the Fates, it is not unusual to direct the feelings at those close by! In addition, she was told that, upon her husband's asking what the psychiatrist had said (he knew that she was keeping the appointment), he should be told that the speculation was made regarding the mourning and that the psychiatrist wanted to speak to *him* further about it. The woman went home after her appointment and may or may not have told him this, as she had become so bewildered by what was happening. At the next appointment (again hopefully the husband was to come), she arrived with her daughter. Her husband had meanwhile been encouraged to phone his regular physician, have his blood sugar level checked, resumed his medication for diabetes, and been told by his physician: "Yes, you should see the psychiatrist!" Further, the daughter confirmed that the mother *had* told the husband after the first appointment of our conversation.

What then? What else was to be done? As the spouse seemed too fatigued and bewildered to carry on the rescue efforts alone, I strongly recommended to the daughter that she and *her* husband accompany the father to the next appointment and, should he refuse, tell him that an ambulance would be provided and hospitalization obtained. Follow-through was to take place! The day before the scheduled appointment, on reflecting over what had already transpired, I decided to take an even more active role. I telephoned the family, determined to speak with the husband himself. His wife answered and got her husband to the phone. I indicated that, having met his wife and daughter, I was concerned for him and that I could appreciate there were many emotions going on, especially since the illness of his sibling. His response was that the sibling situation contributed but was not the whole story. Yet he admitted being "confused." At that point, I stated it takes a big person to acknowledge confusion and that I looked forward to meeting him in person the following day, whether accompanied or not accompanied by his family!

Orchestration of a rescue by several people had to be employed. One could imagine that the self-destructive feelings had become so intense that suicide might well have ocurred at any point if the rescue efforts had shown any degree of waning. The wife's efforts had almost sapped her strength. When first seen, she had been trembling and tearful and wanted me to write down the supposition about mourning so that she would not forget what was being said—so distraught had she become at her seeming inability to ward off her husband's impending suicide. Fortunately, she had turned to her daughter and son-in-law, who could then share in the rescue efforts *before* she alone might have failed her husband. They in turn mobilized efforts of two professionals, the family physician, known by the potential victim, and the psychiatrist. By sheer weight of the rescuers, the wishes for self-destruction were tenuously being overriden by the wishes to live. The word *tenuously* has to be kept in mind, for it so well conveys the nip-and-tuck survival of such a man. In addition, the word *tenuously* conveys to the reader the frequent needs of the rescuer(s) to be alert, not to be worn down, and to be consistent in all the rescue efforts transmitted back to the potential suicide victim.

LEGITIMACY OF HELP

Another true story highlights once again how pride of the suicide person continues being a potential lethal factor even after the wishes for rescue have been delivered and received. I have discussed how pride may obscure the message to be rescued in the first place. But to realize that pride and repercussions thereof remain operating *after* the rescue has been initiated needs further emphasis. A patient I had known for several years, but whom I had not seen for some time, once again called and asked to consult. Work circumstances, with current disappointment regarding what seemed to have been a promised promotion not delivered, had stimulated once again all the previous feelings of unworthiness, depression, and anger that augured poorly for survival. Talking once more in an office setting hopefully would help reestablish equilibrium. The new set of events were described, and some measure of relief was obtained during the hour. At the conclusion, I suggested, that even though he was constructively trying to work things out and felt some optimism, I would like to hear from him in the next couple of days. About three days later, he called in the morning, stating he was with his wife and could they come in and see me later that day. Arrangements were made. The man had made a severe suicide attempt in the past when I originally cared for him. And he did not have to wave many more flags or posters before my eyes. That late afternoon while in my office, the three of us (his spouse, too) agreed to hospitalization, and I called and made the necessary arrangements. He subsequently asked his wife to leave the office a moment in order to tell me how horribly depressed he had become, including having fleeting ideas of killing his wife and children in order that they would not have to suffer being left alone if he killed himself *only*. "I know I would never do anything like that, Dr. Berent, but just having thoughts like that..."

At any rate, the following morning in the hospital, we had another meeting. And I was bewildered! And also felt a little annoyed! My patient was recounting circumstances of his life in chronological order that covered his past leading to his current admission. Approximately 99% of the material I had heard before. I was beginning to think my still young (early forties) patient was having senile changes, as he seemed to be so repetitive. Our interview concluded, and it was decided I would see him regularly but not the next day (Sunday). I remarked to my wife about the unusual experience I had had with the man, and her response was: "He was just telling you and himself *why* he had to be in the hospital!" Of course! So simple. He needed to convince the proud part of himself that his admission was for genuine reasons. A patient with a broken leg or x-ray evidence of pneumonia can legitimately be placed in a hospital. Anyone can see the obvious necessity for that! But the patient with emotional problems? How can he display his "legitimacy?" Was not this man's recital of his history *his* way of asking once again for my sanctifying the decision we had made? Did he have to jump from a building or swallow a near-fatal dose of drugs to be legitimate in his claim for help? I understood this several hours after the fact. The following morning, the patient called me at home from the hospital. He was feeling better and wanted to be discharged. He knew with what he had to deal. Looking around the hospital, he saw people worse off than himself—who had "real problems"—and now he would go home and manage. Indeed, he had met some other patients whose parents had suicided and knew he could not do that to his family. My response was to state that I wanted him to remain there; other people might be seen as more obviously needing help, but I knew that his feelings were equally strong, although perhaps not worn on his sleeve; yes, he was a voluntary patient and could demand his release, but I felt he should stay for a while. "Okay! Since you want me to stay, I'll stay!"

RESCUER'S EXPECTED PERFECTION

By this time, the reader can appreciate a few parallels to the 7:30 AM patient. However, I had been better prepared to deal with the preceding man. The issues of shame and pride were so outstanding that he could be relieved only be my making a strong statement that he remain. My flagging interest the previous day and my annoyance based on some miscomprehension of his recital were perceived at least subliminally by the patient. Here I had first complied with the necessity of his being hospitalized and only 24 hours later could emanate something less than fully positive in my rescue efforts. His telephone call to me the following morning should be understood as his rechecking me to see if, indeed, I *really* cared enough for him, that his hospitalization had been legitimate. If I had readily agreed to his discharge or only with moderate protest, it would have been confirmation of what he sensed (or felt he sensed) during our preceding meeting. The person in overwhelming crisis expects perfection of his rescuer. There is no consideration that I, his rescuer, could have an off day, one in which I would not be exactly on target and comprehend his every communication precisely. True, as a professional, that is what I am being paid to do, however! But professionals, too, are human beings and, by definition, not perfect. Tragically, the suicide person does not understand this as he relates to his rescuer. And such "lapses of perfection" could easily be experienced once again as rejection. To understand this demand for perfection, we once more need to consider the original rescue model described in the first chapter. The infant is fused with his parent-rescuer. Omnipotence and/or magic is shared. Later in adult life, the relics of this magic are placed into the hands of rescuers during overwhelming crisis. It is the nature of such crisis that we can be thrust back into time in such a fashion.

Individuals who work in psychiatric hospitals, including nurses, psychiatric aides, and doctors, are continually being tested as to the authenticity of their positive responses to the suicidal person or being asked to verify the legitimacy of the latter's hospitalization. These points and their significance make certain acts by some suicidal persons while hospitalized more comprehensible. What I have in mind are specific repeated tendencies to inflict injury on themselves. Breaking light bulbs to use the glass to cut their wrists, or throats, for example, represents one of the devices employed that on occasion threaten to end life. Again, when the action is not understood by the staff (would-be rescuers) as a symbolic plea to have acknowledged the seriousness and legitimacy of the suicide person's dilemma, a crescendo of similar acts occurs. Meanwhile, staff can become angry, feel convinced manipulation is going on, retaliate by restricting activities (e.g., phone calls, visiting privileges) for the safety of the patient. Such cyclic "games" between staff and patient have to end as stalemate at best and in death at worst. Shock therapy, additional or changed medication would not replace the needed ingredient of being successfully reassured of legitimacy of hospitalization in the first place. When this concept is firmly established for the patient and staff, proceeding successfully with therapy is assured. Yet, again, even within the course of one hospitalization, a patient needs repetition of this reassurance. To the degree this can be given before the patient is made to clamor for it, more exasperated, frustrated requests bordering on complete self-destruction can be avoided. It is *not* necessarily masochism that has the suicide person repetitively making progressive attempts on his life.

Description of what is required of rescuers in the hospital is not so different in kind from what is necessary of rescuers on a follow-through regime out of the hospital. The intensities may be different, with margin of error perhaps larger within the hospital, where the suicide person may have a multitude of rescuers available. And if one does not quite come through, perhaps another rescuer might. This gets us back to consideration of the first case in this chapter. Whether the locale is inside or outside of a psychiatric setting, the rescuer is energetically challenged to fulfill his role. All things being equal, the outside rescuers are at a disadvantage in that the role is new to them and the expectations likewise are not familiar. When placed in such an unfamiliar role that can no longer be put aside, anxiety increases. To see clearly that one's spouse is becoming progressively morose and not be able to turn the tide has to be frightening, confusing, and demoralizing. The woman whom I earlier described was essentially a bright woman but had been reduced to a barely functional one, as her impotence at succeeding with her husband was becoming clear. As mentioned, she was able to enlist help from her daughter, son-in-law, and physician and eventually a successful outcome could evolve.

But let's for a moment consider another type of situation—again, a desperate spouse fearing the potential suicide of a loved one who will not voluntarily seek additional help. There are no daughters or sons-in-law to call. What then? Call one's neighbors? Police? Fire department? Nearest psychiatric hospital? Psychiatrist from the yellow pages of the telephone directory? Any and all would be legitimate. It is not only a crisis for the suicide person but also a crisis for the rescuer, who may have been receiving clues for some time and gradually been succumbing to the emotional depletion of anxiety, not knowing what to do, and general impotence. The rescuer, when forced to enlist others to become part of a rescue team, should also be taken quite seriously, even if the resultant appearance is somewhat hysterical and confused. A neighbor, who might respond by saying "Calm down, Mrs. Jones, your husband's a bit depressed but everything is going to be O.K.!'' will have missed the point completely. Indeed, I have been told the story of a woman who called the police when her husband was suicidal and when they came appeared so upset that they believed her cool, composed husband's story—namely, the woman was the person needing hospitalization. And shortly after *her* hospitalization, the husband shot himself. This is a true story and not a take off of Thurber's *A Unicorn in the Garden,* in which a husband tells his wife there's a unicorn in the garden and, when she calls the ''little men in white,'' the husband denies seeing such an animal, stating it must be something strange with his wife. The wife is taken to the asylum and Thurber concludes: ''Don't count your boobies until they are hatched!'' I don't have such a clever punch line for my story. Nor do I have a ready solution for avoiding such mistakes. All of us would wish to have crystal balls and be perfect in our predictions and evaluations. In lieu of such perfection, we still strive for the ideal.

In concluding this chapter, I wish to dispel some of the possible pessimism engendered by relating the above material. By and large, the role of rescuer need not be as difficult as presented in these last several pages. I do not mean to imply that it is easy. But ordinarily, one does not have to go to such extremes to accomplish successful connection with the suicidal person. I do not want to frighten the potential rescuer reader away. On the other hand, I would have felt myself remiss if I did not at least indicate some of the problems the rescuer may have once he has accepted the role.

To briefly summarize this section: The rescuer, even after recognition of his role with the suicide person, must continually be aware of the latter's pride. Even though one has temporarily become dependent on the services of a rescuer, pride still remains. Perhaps such sensitivity is even increased. Similarly, attention to confirming the legitimacy of the suicide person's receiving help must consistently be given. A measure of repetition may be necessary if not the general rule. Recognizing that the suicidal person is demanding that the rescuer be perfect, at least from his or her more primitive longings mobilized by the extreme overwhelmed position, it might be helpful to admit one's imperfections. For example, one might say something to the effect that: "I really want to help and *understand,* but I may not always be on target. You may have to explain certain things to me a couple times." Such statements would not be contrived nor artificial. They happen to describe accurately what characterizes the usual situation. And, incidentally, it helps the suicidal person realize he is not competing with some alleged God. In a roundabout way, the suicidal person begins to recognize his *own* contribution to the rescue process. In this regard, I like to mention that at the next session I told my patient, the one who gave his recital of circumstances leading to hospitalization, of my initial failure to fully comprehend the previous meeting. Actually, I even spoke of my concern that he might have sensed my inner irritation. His response was: "Oh! I know you are concerned, Dr. Berent. But I did notice that you seemed more anxious to complete and leave our meeting than usual. Though, perhaps, you had to hurry and make your other commitments." Basically, he handled my apology graciously and continued to take more energetic responsibility for his own rescue. Had I not made my acknowledgment, our relationship might have been jeopardized rather than strengthened. Subsequent to this point, we could get on with his therapy. The rescue process had proceeded beyond the initial follow-through. The sense of commitment had been reestablished. He had a right to his misery. But he also had a right to live and see alternatives. The seal of legitimacy had been conveyed.

As I rethink the above, a few additional comments about depression help embellish the concept of legitimacy. First of all, it takes a great deal of honesty to acknowledge one's depression. All sorts of maneuvers may have been used formerly by a person to ward off such sensations. Alcoholism is an obvious camouflage. Anger and hate similarly, when directed at others, may spare a person comparable feelings toward himself. A whole array of techniques (classically call-ed mechanisms of defense) might be utilized to avoid painful awareness that constitute depression. The potential rescuer, when observing the above behavior easily may miss the underlying depression, having been taken in by the camouflage. Similarly, even if the underlying depression is picked up, the approach to the potential victim often is made difficult by the latter's denial of his feelings. A case in point follows:

Some time ago, again after giving a lecture about suicide, a person in the audience raised this pertinent ques-tion: "I have a 22-year-old friend who sincerely wishes to die young (by 30). His father died in a car crash when my friend was four, and his best friend died in a car crash when he was 19. His mother is a very weak figure [A poor or tired rescuer, in our terms] in his life, and for several years now, he's led an extremely self-destructive life. He's nearly killed himself several times in car accidents and with drugs. How does one rescue a person like this?" The answer: with difficulty! Seriously, to the degree my questioner could feel greater strength and conviction about her role as rescuer, she might more effectively approach her friend with her recognition of the legitimacy of his depression. Rather than emphasize to him the outward show of his self-destructive acts (i.e., car crashes and drugs), perhaps she could cut through to the heart of the matter: "You lost your father and then your best friend in car crashes. You have a *right* to be depressed! It's *legitimate*! Don't run away from the feelings. It's alright to have tears. You don't have to be a hard guy!" Admittedly, the situation is a most difficult one—namely, getting this suicidal person to acknowledge his depression to himself let alone to another person.

On the other hand, when the suicidal person *does* admit to his feelings of depression, this actually is an advance toward health. He has put aside various veneers and is now at his true essence. For the would-be rescuer to then respond with "Oh! It's okay. Everything will be alright. Don't you worry!" is failing to recognize another aspect of his follow-through functions. He is inadvertently trying to cover over the depressed feelings which the depressed person has so laboriously finally unmasked to himself. What irony! Instead, the proper position for the rescuer is to provide ample time for ventilation of the feelings. Anything less would be an affront. Such comments as "everything will be alright" could be construed by the suicidal person as having taken his situation lightly. Once more, this lends itself to a sense of rejection. Not being understood or having one's feelings minimized is like a powder keg. The desperate person, once he is speaking of his depressed feelings, does not necessarily expect his listener to immediately step in and offer suggestions or condolences. The process of dialogue with a minimum of interjections by the listener is appropriate for the beginning. A connection to another person is being established, even though, at first, a subtle one. Respect, too, is thereby conveyed back to the suicidal person by his listener, who is not too quick to barge in with panaceas. Legitimacy of the person's feelings is a feedback from his listener that is crucial. There is a fine line of difference that I am trying to demarcate. I am *not* saying it is legitimate to commit suicide. I *am* saying that it is legitimate to have depressed feelings. In fact, I wonder if the act of suicide itself is not a final maneuver to avoid fully encompassing and acknowledging the caldron of depression, hate, anger, frustration—all of which have stewed in juices unattended by one's greater consciousness, becoming a self-poisoning witches' brew. The rescuer's function of stressing the legitimacy of the suicidal person's predicament does not change the predicament, but it may help neutralize some of the poison. This alteration itself may help the person achieve his own solutions, sharing the role of being his own rescuer in the most positive fashion.

Chapter 10

THE ALGEBRA OF SUICIDE— A
MATHEMATICAL SUMMARY

On contemplating the best ways of summarizing this book, it
has dawned on me that an algebraic point of view may help
condense and put in order the relevance of the rescuer in
suicide.

If we begin with the following notations

Sp = suicide potential
Vm = victim's motivation
Ra = rescuer's availability

we have the necessary ingredients for the first partial equa-
tions A and B.

EQUATION A. $Sp \sim Vm$. Basically, this states that suicide
potential is in direct proportion to the victim's motivation.
By and large, writers about suicide have confined their work
and limited their interpretation of statistics to the issue of
motivation. Suicide profiles are established:

1. more apt to be male than female
2. more apt to be older male
3. more apt to be single...and so on.

These profiles are fine as far as they go, but they often give rise to misconceptions that detract from their value even at that. For example, the use of statistics to demonstrate that more males actually commit suicide whereas more females make suicide attempts conveys a sense that different diseases are being discussed rather than properly showing the spectrum of motivation on a continuum, where to communicate with a potential rescuer is more compatible with pride (ego syntonic) for the woman in our culture. Even in our days of women's liberation, it still remains more permissible to be dependent on a potential rescuer if you are a woman. Granted this greater permission to seek a rescuer, the Vm (victim's motivation) is of a different magnitude. And this has value only when large numbers are being considered. With any specific woman (as with any man or child), to rely on the above partial equation alone is foolhardy.

EQUATION B. $\quad Sp \simeq \dfrac{1}{Ra}$

Obviously, my book has included emphasis on this second partial equation, which basically connotes that suicide potential is in *inverse* proportion to the rescuer's availability. Some elements that contribute to the rescuer's availability have in part been illustrated (e.g., the wearing out of the rescuer).

EQUATION C. $\quad Sp = \dfrac{Vm}{Ra}$

This third simplified equation combines the preceding two. The meaning would be as follows: suicide potential is directly proportional to the victim's motivation *and* inversely proportional to the rescuer's availability.

Now, if applying algebra to human behavior could be as exact as applying algebra to some aspects of chemistry, I could stop now with this algebra lesson. And, if I did, readers who may have been unsuccessful rescuers could all jump off bridges with their guilt. For, algebraically, they no longer could deny their role in the suicide happening. They had missed the boat. The rationale for why a book of this sort has not been published becomes very clear: rather than preventing suicides, it would increase suicides among the surviving rescuers, who would have seen themselves as such horrible failures.

But the algebra lesson is not yet complete. Additional refinements of Equation C actually may help reduce this issue of guilt in the rescuer-survivor. At least, a more complete perspective is needed. To paraphrase an old adage, ''Beauty is in the eye of the beholder,'' we need to consider that love (or hate) is also in the eye of the beholder. Translated into suicide terms, I am saying that the idea of rescue or not being rescued is in the mind of the potential victim. Algebraically, the notation Ra (rescuer's availability) needs to be subdivided into at least two categories:

1. *Rav* rescuer's availability in the mind of the victim
2. *Rao* rescuer's availability in the *outer* ''real'' world.

Equation C can now be modified to the following:

$$\text{EQUATION D.} \qquad Sp = \frac{Vm}{Rav + Rao}$$

Equation D comes closer to approximating the suicide relationships. For the reader now can see that the rescuer is made up of the two ingredients, the rescuer as perceived by the potential victim and the ''real'' rescuer. It does not take too much imagination to realize that the *perceived* rescuer does not qualitatively nor quantitatively always coincide with the *real* rescuer. The "poison" (e.g., LSD, angel dust, alcohol, "erosion of the spirit," etc.) that colors the sensorium of the potential victim can well make devils of would-be real rescuers and, vice-versa, gods out of the poorest rescuer symbols. When the chips are down, the well-intentioned enlightened real rescuer can only hope to influence constructively the rescuer image in the mind of the potential victim. And, as I have emphasized, this rescuer image may have been in the making for years; or the converse: the rescuer image may have been eroded during the years!

Once again, algebraically, it could be looked at this way: *Rav* does not necessarily equate in prominence with *Rao*. *Rav* far surpasses *Rao* in importance for survival. Equation D has to be altered to indicate this proposition. If we place *Rav* and *Rao* in brackets with exponents x and y, where x is significantly greater than y, we can evolve

Equation E:

$$\text{Berent's Law} \quad Sp = \frac{Vm}{[Rav]^x + [Rao]^y}$$

Although this algebra has been presented tongue in cheek, I hope seriously to have conveyed step by step a more objective way of viewing the rescuer's role. We in the "outer world" of the potential suicide victim may represent his or her last vestige of hope that is to do battle with the death wishes otherwise existing and being influenced by the diminishing availability of the rescuer within the victim's inner world. And, in spite of our efforts, we may be misperceived.

Misperceived? The human element has so much paradox and irony. It is no wonder that we often turn for solace to mathematics, where answers *seem* simple, concise, and stable. But even that may be an illusion. For once one gets beyond $2 + 2 = 4$, even seemingly simple chemical formulas prove not so simple. Take, for example, the equation $2H_2 + O_2 \rightleftharpoons 2H_2O$. Chemists tell us that things are not so simple as we might wish. Instead, they would point out to us that a closer approximation of the truth would be expressed as follows: $2H_2 + O_2 = 2H_2O$. There is a system in operation in which two molecules of H_2 and one molecule of O_2 are in equilibrium with two molecules of water. The reactions are going both ways—the prominance of one direction over the other being dependent on other factors.

Confusion? To say the least! And confusion occuring in "simple" situations to boot. How much more confusion are the roles of suicidal victim and rescuer when seen in the following true-life "system."

The Story of Mad Miriam

A number of years ago two sisters 18 and 20 years of age had been living together when the younger one committed suicide. I knew neither of them and so cannot describe the grief of the survivor let alone the circumstances surrounding the suicide. However, the older sister subsequently married and had a daughter whom she named after the deceased sister. This daughter, whom I'll call Miriam, came to consult with me when she was a young woman in her twenties. She was depressed and had been so for some years. What she found remarkable were occasions when she was out with friends and found herself smiling or laughing and then "caught" herself, once more becoming somber if not depressed. We were both puzzled by this, until her report of a weekend spent with her mother offered a possible explanation. Her mother had been drinking heavily, which was not so unusual. What was odd for the patient was that she felt that her mother, when addressing her, was actually talking to her deceased aunt. "I know our names are the same, but there was something different. She's called me Miriam all my life. But this was different. I was her sister, not her daughter.

We were beginning to see how some of the puzzle was coming together. Her mother had been an unsuccessful rescuer, and the daughter, by substituting for the depressed aunt, was giving her mother another chance at being a rescuer—to undo the tragedy of the past. My patient, obviously in need of rescue herself with her severe depression, was simultaneously a rescuer to her mother by providing the mother an opportunity to rescue her rather than drinking herself to death.

mother rescuer of daughter (sister)
$$\xrightarrow{\hspace{3cm}}$$
(a system)
$$\xleftarrow{\hspace{3cm}}$$
mother rescued by daughter

Interblending of roles in a fluid system may not be so unusual. Indeed, when seen in this context of rescuer and suicide victim, the question of familial and/or genetic causes of suicide can be placed in better perspective. We do not have to presuppose genetic weak links and hereditary taints. Our germ plasm or DNA are not the most likely explanations for a tendency toward suicides in families. It is just much more likely that we have had systems like Mad Miriam's family in which roles of victim and rescuer can be replayed, interchanged with enough opportunities for successful suicides to fuel the energies of subsequent systems in succeeding generations.

Chapter 11

A MORE CONVENTIONAL SUMMARY

WISH TO BE RESCUED EMPHASIZED AGAIN

Over and over again, I have stressed this wish to be rescued to the point of seeming like a broken record. Granted, the wish may come across very disguised, "magical," or scrambled and we may then miss it. Like the suicidal person, the rescuer is also a human being—and, by definition, not perfect. But as mentioned earlier, to strive for the ideal is also typically human.

And what is the value of recognizing the wish to be rescued? The answer is simply: time. The recognition itself does not cure the situation. We have not changed the dynamics of frustration, anger, and depression altogether. But we may have just by our recognition of the impending crisis of the suicidal person given time a chance to work favorably. Our intervention is already something new for the patient. It is a spark of interest in what otherwise is complete despair. The sigh of relief in the would-be suicidal patient has been seen by many therapists. The young military cartoonist with his drawings whom I described earlier, epitomizes the point. His tears at my confrontation were tears of relief. I am not being melodramatic when I emphasize that I shall always remember him. But the most significant thing for the reader to remember is that his situation is not really all that unique. Others want to be confronted—need to be confronted—must be confronted. *Dead is dead*. Regrets, could-have-beens, and so on are all that linger if we have not been able to interpose time. Enough time! With time, the sense of being overwhelmed may be gradually replaced by reemerging strengths of the suicidal person, alternate perspectives, and a renewed sense of connection to another person. Time does not cure everything. But it helps! Old cliches may still have their relevance.

Trusting One's Intuition as a Rescuer

Feminine intuition could itself be the subject of a book. The ramifications of why intuition (and feelings) have been assumed to be the sole province of women are intriguing. Starting from infancy, a boy in this country gets programmed to think that it is not manly to cry and let his feelings be known. To a lesser degree, even little girls experience this injunction, too. Obviously, this has been an extra handicap both for the male suicidal person as well as for the male rescuer. In this context, we might speculate that the higher rate of successful suicides among males may be a reflection of their poorer ability to communicate their feelings in the first place. And the male rescuer? He, too, may have a tendency to have blunted awareness of feelings. His receptors may atrophy from disuse! Hopefully, when women's liberation has reached its goals, a men's liberation may evolve, in which men will have equal rights to exhibit and sense their own feelings. That society will grant full recognition and legitimacy to males possessing feeling is to be hoped.

In all seriousness, intuition is to be trusted. It is amazing how our minds, almost in a subliminal way, register the incoming stimuli (rescue messages) and produce sensations of vague discomfort—all's not well! Too often we are apt to let these sensations pass. But don't. There is really no danger that I know of in overreacting, reading a suicide message when it really does not exist. The worst that can happen is that the person whom we have judged as possibly suicidal will smile and reassure us. His smile is a thankfulness that we are really so interested. Our expressed concern will not drive him over the brink into suicide. Such individuals may compose a group of people who live because we have intervened. We may never know how meaningful our confrontation has been. And so we may tend to minimize it. We do not have a statistical way of enumerating the lives that have been rescued in such a group. Statistically, we are more apt to know only those who died.

What else can we say about intuition? Oversimplified though this definition may be, perhaps it summarizes intuition best: intuition is often the registering in the mind of something out of the ordinary. In regard to suicidal persons, let's review just a few things "out of the ordinary." Besides cartoons like "Help Stamp Out Mental Health," the rope of Mr. X, the 7:30 A.M phone call asking for an appointment, what other kinds of things might register? How about the aggressiveness or sullenness of the military cartoonist? Indeed, that was his manner of presentation to those in authority who initially arranged his hospitalization. What was his original personality like? Literally, I don't know more than that he was a quiet, good boy. "Change in personality" often is a phrase used to describe warning signs. But what about a 16-year-old boy whose parents discover from school authorities that he has been truant for 16 days (a boy who in elementary school was described as an A student). How do you as parents of such a youngster respond? "I'm going to *ground* you for the next upteen weekends! I'm going to take away your allowance! I'm going to...I'm going to!!" Tom

Sawyer and Huckleberry Finn may have enjoyed their truancies, but such was not the case of the young man above. Elaboration of *where* he spent his time (usually at *home* while his parents were at work), with *whom* (usually *alone*—''or once in a while meet some other kid at a drugstore''), or *how* he felt (usually *bored*) reveals a rather upset youngster, to say the least. Suicidal? One has to wonder, or at least explore! Without any reticence, the young man readily accepted the idea of speaking with a psychiatrist when his parents presented him with the opportunity.

Out-of-the-ordinary examples could fill several volumes. But again, just to list them, even in encyclopedia fashion, would perhaps have the adverse reaction on the prospective rescuer-reader of amassing so much material that his intuitive feelings would get crunched in the process. So I have contented myself with just a reminder or two. Let our intuitions be unencumbered!

LONG RANGE NEEDS

A constant task is diagnosing and treating underlying personality traits and fantasies that contribute to vulnerability and lowered thresholds to being overwhelmed, leading to consequent suicide. This aspect of therapy has *not* been the subject of this book. Instead, keeping the patient alive with time for therapy, has been my emphasis. You cannot work with a dead patient. In the beginning of therapy, this principle has to be kept especially in mind. If the first contacts with the patient have given us time in the sense that the patient is responding to us and shows more quick resilience, we may feel safe in seeing the patient in our offices. On the other hand, certain patients require the protective setting of a hospital until enough time has passed in which some of the above criteria are met. Space might be considered another important concept in this context. If hospitalization could be considered another environment away from the one in which the patient has felt overwhelmed we might see it as offering him the opportunity of seeing his problems from afar. Rather than being lost in a forest where he can only see the trees, he is taken out where he can see the whole forest. From a distance (in the hospital or, in less tense situations, in the therapist's office) and with the advantage of time, the ability to locate new solutions is enhanced.

TELL ME I AM NOT A MONSTER!

The angers and hostilities present in the suicidal person, partly due to their feelings of rejection by specific individuals or experienced in more global ways, create a further snowballing effect. On some level, the awareness of one's own hate and venom proves ghastly to the possessor. It becomes convincing proof that all other ugly thoughts about oneself in the past and present are true—only too true. At such a stage, the equivalent to dousing oneself in gasoline and lighting the match has been reached. The cry for help might at this point be: "Please tell me that I'm not a monster!" Actually, if the message is not grasped, and the suicide person completes his act of death, perhaps in some symbolic way he is atoning simultaneously for the angers and hates he is depositing on the heads of his survivors—he effects his own punishment. And a final one!

Douglas Bond, M.D., has written an interesting article on *Frankenstein* and his creator, Mary Shelley.[3] Shelley's mother died in childbirth. Feeling responsible, in the ensuing years Shelley was seen trying desperately to make amends and obtain the love and forgiveness of her father. Bond does well in showing how Frankenstein's ugliness was externally placed (with basic wishes to be loving lying within) to be compared

[3]The Bride of Frankenstein. *Psychiatric Annals* 1973. *3*(12): pp. 10-12.

with Shelley's internalized ugliness. She saw the mere fact of her living as visible proof of the hideous crime she had committed in just being born! The feedback received from her environment (her father) included vibrations not altogether conducive to good mental health!

Such personal myths are not limited only to Mary Shelley. I have had certain patients who felt that they, too, had harmed their mothers in childbirth (not actually killing them) to such an extent that their subsequent lives were spent in atoning in one fashion or another. The point is that many individuals have developed their own private myths about themselves from a variety of sources in which the result has them perpetually questioning their worth, requiring excessive reassurance that they are not actually monsters. These themes, even when not obviously operative, may lie dormant only to rise to the surface at some new external stimulus and prove the dominating force leading to the state of being overwhelmed. The repetitive ways these themes may be played during life are endless. As mentioned much earlier in the book, the fairy tale of Snow White (Mirror, mirror on the wall—who is the fairest of them all?) is the epitome of the universality of this need to be reassured that I'm not a witch and monster. As children, we have all responded to this story. It hit a nerve! Hopefully, most of us have dealt with our hates well enough or had reassurances strong enough to allow ourselves some measure of contentment and self-worth that sustains us. As humans, we are not angels. But neither are we monsters!

NOTHING SO NEW

"The Fantasy of Being Rescued in Suicide" by Viggo Jensen and Thomas Petty represented a concise presentation to the professional reader and to their students, of which I am one. This book is essentially an elaboration for more general consumption. Themes and ideas have had their predecessors through the generations and centuries. What is valuable is the emphasis and reintegration, perhaps in new formats, for new readers of some old ideas. When it gets down to it, the wish to be rescued and clues to suicide have been essentially known to the ancients and poets of all times. Over 2,000 years ago, Sophocles in his *Oedipus Rex*[4] has Choragos, spokesman of the Chorus, saying the following to the hero, Oedipus (regarding the latter's wife): "Why has she left us, Oedipus? Why has she gone in such a passion of sorrow? I fear this silence: Something dreadful may come of it." (Scene III) In the Exodos, Sophocles has a messenger announce the death of the queen to the same Choragos who responds: "Jocaste? Dead? But at whose hand?" The messenger replies: "Her own. The full horror of what happened you can not know, for you did not see it; but I, who did, will tell you as clearly as I can how she met her death."

There is seeing, and there is *seeing!* The author expresses a sense of irony in that the minor character originally senses something is amiss in the demeanor of the queen only to act as if he were dumbfounded later by the news of the suicide. He has had to deny to himself that which he had experienced just shortly before. Sophocles knew about these things.

Perhaps a bit more contemporary, Shakespeare also manages to convey his knowledge of suicide with Lady Macbeth. In Act V, Scene I, a doctor, a woman attendant, and Lady Macbeth are portrayed, the latter being observed by the other two. As a somnambulist, Lady Macbeth reveals her sins to her rescuers. Her hand-washing ceremonies have been observed ("Here's the smell of the blood still: all the

Dudley Fitts, editor: *Four Greek Plays,* New York. Harcourt, Brace & World, Inc. 1960.

perfumes of Arabia will not sweeten this little hand...").
Her state of mind has been well perceived by both her woman
attendant and the doctor, who closes the scene:

> Foul whisperings are abroad: unnatural deeds
> Do breed unnatural troubles: infected minds
> To their deaf pillows will discharge their secrets:
> More needs she the divine than the physician.
> God, God forgive us all! Look after her;
> Remove from her the means of all annoyance,
> And still keep eyes upon her. So good night:
> My mind she has mated and amazed my sight:
> I think, but dare not speak.

The physician has received the messages loud and clear. He
even orders the woman attendant to "Remove from her the
means of all annoyance"—namely, any implements that
Lady Macbeth could use to commit suicide. However, his
general attitude is leave her to God! (To hell with her!) She
has so affronted him by what he now knows she has been a
part of that he is in tacit agreement with her woman
attendant, who has also obtained the whole picture. The
agreement is to *make available* the means of suicide, although
dressing it over. Instead of rescuers, they have assumed the
roles of judge and jury. Lady Macbeth dies.

As rescuers, we may be, on occasion, repelled by what
we see. To remain objective when our lives may have been
very much wrapped up with the suicidal person can be an
almost impossible task. Such a task might require the services
of a professional to aid *us* with our care of the desperate person. Fortunately, most suicidal persons do not stimulate our
aversion to the extent of Lady Macbeth! Meanwhile, to be
human is to have feelings. Let us hope that as rescuers we
have strengths that sustain us when the would-be suicide person puts us into his rescue fantasy.

TO THE SUICIDAL PERSON

It may seem ironic that I have addressed this book to your rescuers rather than to you. In fact, you might feel that I have neglected so much of you by emphasizing that small part of you—your wish to live and be rescued. And to the degree that your more self-destructive feelings have not been enlarged upon, such an accusation is quite true. It is not that I have underestimated your suicidal thoughts or your ability to carry them out, but instead, I feel that concentration on your wish to be rescued was, and is, the first order of business.

Consider it from this point of view: the fact that you have looked at this book (or any other book on suicide) may indicate that, in spite of extensive thoughts of death, you may have glimmers of hope to live. These glimmers may be very transient but must be present to some degree. Why otherwise have you bothered with the book? Basically, you are in the act of becoming your own rescuer in the sense of seeking out something from someone that could be utilized to fan these glimmers of hope. That the someone is an author you do not even know—someone, who, therefore, may seem unreal—perhaps offers some protection from the possibility of experiencing yet another hurt were you to once again make an overture toward a person close to you. However subtle, it still seems to me that your wish to live *does* exist and needs more full recognition and acknowledgement by you.

I can anticipate your argument. "Bullshit! I want to die! Don't give me that Pollyanna rubbish!" Again, I am not contradicting your statement that you wish to kill yourself. Yet consider how much pride must be cut through to admit one also might wish to be rescued. All of us take such pride in our independence. Desperation may have prompted some earlier attempts at reaching out. But after a while, when responses were not forthcoming or adequate enough, I could imagine your having become more hurt, angry, isolated, and less inclined than ever to move toward a rescuer. That would be only too human. But then it is also human that our pride can be the death of us. I am not criticizing you for pride. I just know how hard it is to put it aside just in little everyday emotional occurrences. So, believe me, I can imagine clearly just how much pride would have to be swallowed to approach a real-live rescuer. It must be tremendous.

Meanwhile, this pride exists within us and works certain changes on us. It may surprise you! Have you ever thought how your pride affects your appearance! In your convinced position that no one gives a real damn for your feelings, what do you think you look like? Do you think people see your depression, lonely feelings, and desires for contact mixed with fears of ultimate rejection? Do you think they see your hurt at not being fully comprehended? They do not. Often, they just don't see. That's true.

Before I tell you what they may see, let me give you an example of a less life-or-death nature, but one with certain parallels to your situation. Imagine a very shy, awkward person going alone to a dance. The mere fact that he or she is going would be by definition proof that a wish for communication and social interaction exists. But what happens? As a result of anxiety related to anticipating rejection ("No one would really dance with me!"), the person's face and manner take on a withdrawn almost haughty and cold look to the observer—the would-be dance partner or rescuer. Indeed, our shy, awkward person, who may be very warm, sensitive, and beautiful inside, is experienced on the outside as a "cold fish." The would-be rescuer thinks, "Who needs *that* person? He/she has a chip on the shoulder! Seems so cool, controlled, and above it all!"

At this point, I think you must know what I mean. What a paradox! At your time of greatest crisis, when you are most needful of someone responding positively to you, you look like a "cold fish." Your own anticipations of ultimate rejection transform your appearance; your rescuer literally flees from your presence. And so you have made your worst fears come true. No one wants or can stand you. No wonder you want to call it quits. It's the same old story, isn't it?

Yet, wait! Granted that you have been truly hurt or terribly rejected in the past, meeting with insensitivity from others perhaps through no fault of your own, what about *right now!* Are you, because of your fear of rejection, honestly derived from the past, currently making rejectors out of would-be rescuers and friends today? Are you now, and maybe for some time, in the process of creating your own hell? And if you *are* creating your own hell, can you create your own heaven? Life is not a hoax. It is the most important thing you or I have. Neither of us need be involved in heroics to get our messages across to each other. You have suffered a great deal of pain, and I know it. But I do wish you would halt and give yourself more time and space to better determine whether or not you have accidentally contributed to this pain yourself. The total impact of this pain has to be carefully dissected to truly evaluate how much of it is compounded by the new pains we ourselves create with our present-day anticipations.

To be able to take such an objective stance with ourselves is already furthering our role as our own rescuers. Our need for a therapist or outside rescuer to help initiate or to further develop this role of rescuer within us is only human. We do not exist in a vacuum. And to ask for a little bit of encouragement is not really so horrible. Others, too, like to feel needed! As human beings, *all* of us, rescuers and the rescued alike, need this feeling. Things that are so simple still may be true.

SELECTED READINGS

Anderson, D.B., McClean, L.J. *Identifying suicide potential.* New York: Behavioral Publications, 1971.

Cain, Albert, ed. *Survivors of suicide.* Springfield, Ill.: Charles C. Thomas, 1972.

Farberow, Norman L. (Ed.). *The many faces of suicide.* New York: McGraw-Hill, 1980.

Haim, Andre. *Adolescent suicide.* New York: International Universities Press, 1974.

McCulloch, J.W., Philip, A.E. *Suicidal behavior.* New York: Pergamon Press, 1972.

Morgan, Howard G. *Death wishes?* New York: John Wiley & Sons, Ltd, 1979.

Shneidman, Edwin S. (Ed.). *Essays in self-destruction.* New York: Science House, 1967.

Tabachnik, Norman. (Ed.). *Accident or suicide?* Springfield, Ill.: Charles C. Thomas, 1973.

Warren, Max. On suicide. *Journal of the American Psychoanalytic Association,* 1976, 24(1), 199–234.

Wekstein, Louis. *Handbook of suicidology.* New York: Brunner/Mazel, Inc., 1979.

Zusman, J., Davidson, D.L. (Eds.). *Organizing the community to prevent suicide.* Springfield, Ill.: Charles C. Thomas, 1971.

BIBLIOGRAPHY

Acht, E.K. Present status and evaluation of suicide prevention and crisis intervention services in Europe. *Ment. Health Soc.,* 1976, 3(3–4), 169–74.

Allen. N.H. The health education as a suicidiologist, *Suicide Life Threat Behav.,* 1976, 6(4), 195–201.

_____. Suicide survivors: Psychotherapeutic implications of egocide. *Suicide Life Threat Behav.,* 1976, 6(4), 195–201.

Alvarez, A. *The savage god: A study of suicide.* New York: Random House, 1972.

Anstice, E. Dial Mansion House 9000: The Samaritans. *Nurs. Times,* Jan. 27, 1967, 63(4), 123–4.

Atkinson, M. The Samaritans and the elderly: Some problems in communication between a suicide prevention scheme and a group with a high suicide rate. *Soc. Sci. Med.,* Oct. 1971, 5(5), 483–90.

Bagley, C. Suicide prevention: A myth or a mandate? *Br. J. Psychiatry,* July 1973, 123(572), 130.

Bancroft, J.H., Skirmshire, A.M., Simkin, S. The reasons people give for taking overdoses, *Br. J. Psychiatry,* June 1976, 128, 538–48.

Barraclough, B. A medical approach to suicide prevention. *Soc. Sci. Med.,* Dec. 1972, 6(6), 661–7.

Barraclough, B.M., Jennings C. Suicide prevention by the Samaritans: A controlled study of effectiveness, *Lancet,* July 30, 1977, 2(8031), 237–9.

Beck, A.T., Kovacs, M., Weissman, A. Hopelessness and suicidal behavior: An overview, *JAMA,* Dec. 15, 1975, 234 (11), 1146–9.

Beck, R.W., Morris, J.B. Moral attitude and suicidal behavior. *Psychol. Rep.,* June 1974, 34(3), 697–8.

Besel, L. If only the tale had been tattled . . . . *Can. Nurse.,* Oct. 1975, 71(10), 17.

Bidwell, R.E., Bidwell, J.J., Tsai, Sy. Suicide prevention. A study of the community program in Kansas City. *J. Kans. Med. Soc.,* April 1971, 72(4), 167–73, Passim.

Blaker, K. Crisis maintenance, *Nurs. Forum,* 1969, 8(1), 42–9.

Blatt, S.J., Ritzler, B.A. Suicide and the representation of transparency and cross-sections on the Rorschach. *J. Consult. Clin. Psychol.,* Apr. 1974, 42(2), 280–7.

Blomquist, K.B. Nurse, I need help; the school nurse's role in suicide prevention. *J. Psychiatr. Nurs.,* Jan.-Feb. 1974, 12(1), 22–6.

Bray, D.E. Good night, nurse . . . and goodbye . . ., Part I. *J. Pract. Nurs.,* Dec. 1975, 25(12), 16–7, 32.

Cunningham, R. What do nurses do to help patients who attempt suicide? *Can. Nurse,* Jan. 1975, 71(1), 27–9.

Danto, B.L. How to start a suicide prevention center without really trying. *Mich. Med.,* Feb. 1970, 69(3), 119–21.

————. Suicide prevention in Detroit. *Mich. Med.,* Oct. 1970, 69(19), 932.

Day, G. The Samaritan movement in Great Britain. *Perspect. Biol. Med.,* Summer 1974, 17(4), 507–12.

Delbridge, P.M. Identifying the suicidal person in the community. *Can. Nurse,* Nov. 1974, 70(11), 14–7.

Delbruck, M. Education for suicide. *Prism,* 1974, 2, 16–19, 50.

Diran, M.O. You can prevent suicide. *Nursing,* (Jenkintown), Jan. 1976, 6(1), 60–4.

Dorpat, T.L. Drug automatism, barbiturate poisoning, and suicide behavior. *Arch. Gen. Psychiat.,* 1974, 31, 216–220.

Dorpat, T.L., Ripley, H.S. The relationship between attempted suicide and committed suicide, *Comprehensive Psychiat.,* 1963, 4, 117-125.

Draper, D., Margolis, P. A psychodynamic approach to suicide prevention. *Community Ment. Health,* Winter 1976, 12(4): 376-82.

Duncan, J.W. The immediate management of suicide attempts in children and adolescents: Psychologic aspects. *J. Fam. Prac.,* Jan. 1977, 4(1): 77-80.

Eastwood, M.R., Brill, L., Brown, J.H. Suicide and prevention centres. *Can. Psychiatr.. Assoc. J.,* Dec. 1976, 21(8): 571-5.

Eissler, K.R. *The psychiatrist and the dying patient.* New York: International Universities Press, 1955.

Farberow, N.L. *Bibliography on suicide and suicide prevention.* Washton D.C.: National Clearinghouse for Mental Health Information, 1969.

_____. Research in suicide. In: *Suicide prevention in the 70's,* H.L.P. Resnik, (Ed.). Washington, D.C.: Dept. of Health, Education and Welfare, 1973, Pub. No. 72-9054.

_____. Training in suicide prevention for professional and community agents. *Am. J. Psychiatry,* June 1969, 125(12), 1702-5.

Farberow, Norman L., Shneidman, Edwin S., (Eds.). *The cry for help.* New York: McGraw-Hill, preface, p. xi., 1961.

Farberow, N.L. and MacKinnon, D. A suicide prediction schedule for neuropsychiatric hospital patients. *J. Nerv. Ment. Dis.,* June 1974, 158(6), 408-19.

Fawcett, J. Suicidal depression and physical illness. *JAMA,* Mar. 6, 1972, 219(10), 1303-6.

Feigin, R.A. Inception of a 'grass roots' mental health delivery system. pp. 571-5, In: Shephard, R.J., and Itoh, S., (Eds.). *Circumpolar Health.* Toronto: Univ. of Toronto Press, 1976. W3 IN916VE 1974c.

Finlay-Jones, R.A., Kidd, C.B. The clients of the telephone Samaritan service in Western Australia, *Med. J. Aust.,* April 1, 1972, 1(14), 690-4.

Fox, R. Suicide in Brighton, *Br. J. Psychiatry,* Jan. 1973, 122(566), 116.

_____. Today's student. (C): Suicide among students and its prevention. *R. Soc. Health J.,* July-Aug. 1971, 91(4); 181-5.

Frederick, C.J., Farberow, N.L. Group psychotherapy with suicidal persons: A comparison with standard group methods. *Int. J. Soc. Psychiatry,* Spring 1970, 16(2), 103-11.

Frank, A.O. The management of attempted suicide—reflections of a physician. *Med. J. Malaysia,* June 1977, 31(4), 281-4.

Freud, S. The economic problem of masochism. *Standard Edition,* 1924, 19, 157-170. London: Hogarth Press, 1961.

_____. Mourning and melancholia. *Standard Edition,* 1917, 14, 239-258. London: Hogarth Press, 1957.

Friedman, J.S. Cry for help: Suicide in the aged. *J. Gerontol Nurs.,* May-June 1976, 2(3), 28–32.

Friedman, P. (ed.). *On suicide.* New York: International Universities Press, 1967.

Ganguly, H.R. Depression and suicide. *J. Indian Med. Assoc.,* Dec. 16, 1972. 59(12), 525.

Getz, W.L., Fujita, B.N., Skrimshire, A.M. The use of paraprofessionals in crisis intervention: Evaluation of an innovative program. *Am. J. Community Psychol.,* June, 1975, 3(2). 135–44.

Gibson, M.R., Lott, R.S. Suicide and the role of the pharmacist. *J. Am. Pharm. Assoc.,* Sept. 1975, 12(9), 457–61, Passim.

Hartmann, H. Comments on the psychoanalytic theory of the ego. In: *Essays on Ego Psychology,* New York: International Universities Press, 1964, pp. 113–141.

————. On rational and irrational action. (1947) In: *Essays on Ego Psychology.* New York: International Universities Press, 1964, pp. 37–68.

Havens, L.L. The anatomy of a suicide. *New Eng. J. Med.* Feb. 25, 1965, 272, 401–406.

Heath, M. Quiet cries. Can I help? Will you listen? *Nurs. Care,* April 1973, 6(4), 26–30.

Hendin, H. *Suicide and Scandinavia.* New York: Grune & Stratton, 1964.

Hersh, S.P. Suicide: Youth's high vulnerability to it/Signs to look for/ How you can help. *MH,* Summer 1975, 59(3), 23–5.

Herzog, A., Resnik, H.L.P. A clinical study of parental response to adolescent death by suicide with recommendations for approaching survivors. in Farberow, N.L. (ed.): *Suicide and its prevention: Proceedings of the Fourth International Conference for Suicide Prevention.* Los Angeles: Delmar Publishing Co, 1968.

Holding, T.A. The B.B.C. 'Befrienders' series and its effects, *Br. J. Psychiatry,* May, 1974, 124(0), 470–2.

————. Suicide and 'The Befrienders.' *Br. Med. J.,* Sept. 27, 1975, 3(5986), 751–2.

Horoshak, I. How to spot and handle high-risk patients. *RN,* Sept. 1977, 40(9), 58–63.

Horton, P.C. The mystical experience as a suicide preventive. *Am J. Psychiatry,* March 1973, 130(3), 294–6.

Hoxworth, D., Toole, B. A community's answer to the cry for help. *Hosp. Community Psychiatry,* Sept. 1970, 21(9), 296–7.

Imlach, A. Alberta Task Force on suicide problem finds present attitudes inadequate. *Can. Med. Assoc. J.,* Sept. 1976, 115(6), 580–2.

Jensen, V.N. & Petty, T.A. The fantasy of being rescued in suicide. *Psychoanal. Quart.,* 1958, 27; 327–339.

Johnson, F.G., Ferrence, R., Whitehead, P.C. Self-injury: Identification and intervention. *Can. Psychiatr. Assoc. J.,* 1973, 18(2), 101–5.

Kahne, M.J. Suicide among patients in mental hospitals. *Psychiat.,* 1968, 31, 32–43.

Katschnig, H., Steinert, H. The strategic function of attempted suicide. *Ment. Health Soc.,* 1975, 2(3-6), 288–93.

Keen, E. Suicide and self-deception. *Psychoanal Rev.,* Winter 1973, 60(4): 575–85.

Kohut, H. Thoughts on narcissism and narcissistic rage. *The Psychoanalytic Study of the Child,* 1972, 27, 401–410. New York: Quadrangle Books.

Kopell, B.S. Treating the suicidal patient. *Geriatrics,* Sept. 1977, 32(9), 65–7.

Kovacs, M., Beck, A.T., Weissman, A. The communication of suicidal intent. A reexamination. *Arch Gen Psychiatry,* Feb. 1976, 33(2), 198–201.

Krieger, G. The management and mismanagement of a suicidal patient. *Hosp. Community Psychiatry,* June 1976, 27(6), 411–3.

Leonard, C.V. Treating the suicidal patient: A communication approach. *J. Psychiatr. Nurs.,* 1975, 13(2), 19–22.

Lester, D. Attempts to predict suicidal risk using psychological tests. *Psychol. Bull.,* 74(1), 1–17.

_____. Attitudes toward death held by staff of a suicide prevention center. *Psychol. Rep.,* April 1971, 28(2), 650.

_____. Suicide-prevention centers and prevention of suicide. *N. Engl. J. Med.,* 289(7), 380.

Leviton, D. A course on death education and suicide prevention: Implications for health education. *J. Am. Coll. Health Assoc.* 19(4), 217–20.

Light, D.W., Jr. Psychiatry and suicide: The managment of a mistake. *Am. J. Sociol.,* March 1972, 77(5), 821–38.

Litman, R.E. Anti-suicide program conducts controlled study. *Evaluation,* 3(1-2), 36–7.

Litman, R.E., Farberow, N.L. The hospital's obligation toward suicide-prone patients. *Hospitals,* Dec. 16, 1966, 40(24), 64–8 Passim.

Litman, R.E., Tabachnik, N. Fatal one-car accidents. *Psychoanal. Quart.,* 1967, 36, 248–259.

Lourie, R. Suicide and attempted suicide in children and adolescents. *Texas Medicine,* 1967, 63, 58–63.

MacKinnon, D.R., Farberow, N.L. An assessment of the utility of suicide prediction. *Suicide Life Threat Behav.,* Summer 1976, 6(2), 86–91.

Maller, O. Suicide and migration. *ISR Ann Psychiatry,* Spring 1966. 4(1), 67–77.

Maltsberger, J., Buie, D.H. Countertransference hate in the treatment of suicidal patients. *Arch. Gen. Psychiat.,* 1974, 30, 625–633.

Marmor, J. The feeling of superiority: An occupational hazard in the practice of psychotherapy. *Am. J. Psychiatry,* 1953, 110, 370–376.

Martz, B.M. The use of volunteers in a suicide prevention program at a private psychiatric hospital. *Hosp. Community Psychiatry,* Oct. 1974, 25(10), 643, 651.

McClean, L.J. Action and reaction in suicidal crisis. *Nurs. Forum,* 1969, 8(1), 28–41.

_____. The rescue system. *Perspectives in Psychiatric Care,* 1972, 10(4), 173–177.

McGee, R.K. Suicide prevention programs and mental health associations. *Ment. Hyg.,* Jan. 1971, 55(1), 60–7.

Meerloo, J.A.M. *Suicide and mass suicide.* New York: Grune & Stratton, 1962.

Menninger, K.A. *Man against himself.* New York: Harcourt, Brace, and Co, 1938.

Messer, M.H. Suicide prevention: Adlerian contribution. *J. Individ. Psychol.,* May 1973, 29(1), 54–71.

Mintz, R.S. Basic considerations in the psychotherapy of the depressed suicidal patients. *Am. J. Psychother.,* Jan. 1971, 25(1), 56–73.

Morse, S.J. The after-pleasure of suicide. *Brit. Med. Psychol.,* 1973, 46, 227–238.

Motto, J.A. Suicide prevention for high-risk persons who refuse treatment. *Suicide Life Threat. Behav.,* Winter 1976, 6(4), 223–30.

_____. Toward suicide prevention in medical practice. *JAMA,* Nov. 17, 1969, 210(7), 1229–32.

Motto, J.A., and Green, C. Suicide and the medical community. *Arch. Neurol. Psychiat,* Dec. 1958, 80, 776–781.

Murphy, G.E., Wetzel, R.D., Swallow, C.S., McClure, J.N., Jr. Who calls the suicide prevention center: A study of 55 persons calling on their own behalf. *Am. J. Psychiatry,* Sept. 1969, 126(3), 314–24.

Murphy, K.B. Rescue Inc. and the licensed practical nurse. *Am. J. Pract. Nurse,* Jan. 1966, 2(1), 32-4, Passim.

Nelson, G., McKenna, J., Koperno, M., Chatterson, J., Brown, J.H. The role of anonymity in suicidal contacts with a crisis center. *Can. Psychiatr. Assoc. J.,* Oct. 1975, 20(6), 455–9.

Neuringer, C. Methodological problems in suicide research. *J. Consult Psychol.,* 1962, 26, 273–278.

Niccolini, R. Reading the signals for suicide risk. *Geriatrics,* May 1973, 28(5), 71–2.

Nunberg, H., Federn, E., (eds.). *Minutes of the Vienna Psychoanalytic Society,* Vol. II. New York: International Universities Press, 1976.

Offenkrantz, W., Church, E., Vitanza, A. Suicide: A review of the literature, 1945-56. *Internat. Red. Med.,* 1957, 170, 678–683.

Olin, H.S. Psychotherapy of the chronically suicidal patient. *Am. J. Psychother.,* Oct. 1976, 30(4), 570–5.

Pilifant, L., Koutsky, C.D. Suicide prevention in Alaska. *Alaska Med.,* April 1972, 14(2), 41–2.

Pitts, F., Winoukur, G., Steward, M. Psychiatric syndromes, anxiety symptoms, and response to stress in medical students. *Am. J. Psychiatry,* 1961, 118, 833–840. Prevention of Suicide. *Who Public Health Pap,* 1968, 35, 1–84.

Priest, R.G. Recognition of the suicidal patient. *J. Int. Med. Res.,* 1977, 5(1 Suppl), 157–63.

Rao, A.V. Suicide. *J. Indian Med. Assoc.,* June 16, 1968, 68(12), 250–2.

Ramon, S., Bancroft, J.H., Skrimshire, A.M. Attitudes towards self-poisoning among physicians and nurses in a general hospital. *Br. J. Psychiatry,* Sept. 1975, 127, 257–64.

Rapp, M.S. The bleeding limit letter. *Can. Med. Assoc. J.,* April 9, 1977. 116(7), 715.

Resnik, H.L.P. The neglected search for the Suicidococcus contagiosa. *Arch. Environ. Health,* Sept. 1969, 19, 307–309.

————. Urban Problems and Suicide Prevention, editorial. *Amer. J. Psychiat.,* June 1969, 125, 1723.

Resnik, H.L., Sweeney, J., Resnik, A.F. Ed telephone: A lifeline for potential suicides. *RN,* Oct. 1974, 37(10), OR1-2 Passim.

Ringel, E. The presuicidal syndrome. *Suicide Life Threat. Behav.,* Fall 1976, 6(3), 131–49.

Rosenbaum, M., Richman, J. Suicide prevention in the military. *Milit. Med.,* June 1970, 135(6), 500–1.

Rosen, D.H. Suicide survivors: Psychotherapeutic implications of egocide. *Suicide Life Threat. Behav.,* Winter 1976, 6(4), 209–15.

Rotov, M. Death by suicide in the hospital: An analysis of 20 therapeutic failures. *Am. J. Psychother.,* April 1970, 24(2), 216–27.

Russell, A.T., Pasnau, R.D., and Taintor, Z.C. Emotional problems of residents in psychiatry. *Am. J. Psychiatry,* Mar. 1975, 132(3), 263–7.

Sanborn, D.E., 3d., Niswander, G.D., Casey, T.M. The family physician, and suicide prevention. *Am. Fam. Physician,* March 1970, 1(3), 75–8.

Sandler, J., Joffe, W.G. Notes on childhood depression. *Internat. J. Psycho-Anal.,* 1965, 46, 88–96.

Sargent, Douglas A., Jensen, Viggo W., Petty, Thomas A., Raskin, Herbert. Preventing physician suicide: The role of family, colleagues, and organized medicine. *JAMA,* Jan. 10, 1977, 237(2), 143–145.

Schein, H.M., and Stone, A.A. Monitoring and treatment of suicidal potential within the context of psychotherapy. *Compr. Psychiat.,* 1969, 10, 59–70.

————. Psychotherapy designed to detect and treat suicidal potential. *Am. J. Psychiatry,* March 1969, 125(9), 1247–51.

Schrut, A. Some typical patterns in the behavior and background of adolescent girls who attempt suicide. *Amer. J. Psychiat.,* 1969, 125, 243–251.

Schuyler, D. When was the last time you took a suicidal child to lunch? *J. Sch. Health.,* Oct. 1973, 43(8), 504–6.

Schwartz, D.A., Flinn, D.E., Slawson, P.F. Treatment of the suicidal character. *Am. J. Psychother.,* April 1974, 28(2), 194–207.

Schwartz, Donald A. The suicidal character. *Psychiatric Quarterly,* 1979, 51(1), 64–70.

Selkin, James. Rescue fantasies in homicide-suicide. *Suicide and Life-Threatening Behavior,* Summer 1976, 6(2), 79–85.

Senseman, L.A. Attempted suicide in adolescents. Suicide Prevention Center in Rhode Island is an urgent need. *RI. Med. J.,* Aug. 1969, 52(8), 449–1.

Shneidman, E.S. (ed.). *On the nature of suicide.* San Francisco: Jossey-Bass, Inc, 1969.

————. Orientation toward death. In: R.W. White (ed.), *Study of lives.* New York: Atherton Press, 1963.

————. Suicide, lethality, and the psychological autopsy. *Int. Psychiatry Clin.,* 1969, 6(2), 225–50.

Shneidman, Edwin S., Farberow, Norman L., and Litman, Robert E. *The psychology of suicide.* New York: Science House, 1970.

Simmel, E. The doctor game, illness, and the profession of medicine. *Psychoanal. Reader,* 1948, 1, 291–305.

Slorach, J. Suicide as catharsis. *Lancet,* Nov. 4, 1972, 2(784), 971.

Spry, W.B. Prevention of suicide. *Occup. Health* (London), July 1976, 28(7), 354–8.

Stengel, E. Recent progress in suicidal persons: A comparison with standard group methods. *Int. J. Soc. Psychiatry,* June 1970, 16(2), 103–11.

————. *Suicide and attempted suicide.* Baltimore: Penguin Books, 1964.

Sterba, R.F. The formative activity of the analyst. *Internat. J. Psycho-Anal.,* 1944, 25, 146–150.

Stone, A.A. Suicide precipitated by psychotherapy: A clinical contribution. *Amer. J. Psychother.,* 1971, 25, 18–26.

Stringfellow, M.E. Talking about suicide. *Sch. Health Rev.,* 1974, 5(5), 40.

Sudac, H.S., Sawyer, J.B., Spring, G.K., and Coakwell, C.M. High referral success rates in a crisis center. *Hosp. Community Psychiatry,* July 1977, 28(7), 530–2.

Suicide and its prevention. *Who Chron.,* Nov. 1968, 22(11), 489–91.

Sumner, F.C., Gwozdz, T.A. A nurse for suicidal patients. *Am. J. Nurs.,* Nov. 1976, 76(11), 1792–3.

Swanson, W.C. Anti-suicide service in New Orleans. *J. LA State Med. Soc.,* March 1971, 123(3), 83–90.

Tabachnick, N. The crisis treatment of suicide. *Calif. Med.,* June 1970, 112(6), 1–8.

Tabachnick, N., Klugman, D. Anonymous suicidal telephone calls: A research critique. *Psychiatry,* Nov. 1970, 33(4), 526–32.

Tarrant, B. Report on the crisis intervention and suicide prevention centre for greater Vancouver. *Can. J. Public Health,* 1970, 61(1), 66–7.

Thomas, C.B. Suicide among us: Can we learn to prevent it? *Johns Hopkins Med. J.,* Nov. 1969, 125(5), 276–85.

_____. What becomes of medical students: The dark side. *Johns Hopkins Med. J.,* May 1976, 138(5), 185–95.

Waggoner, R.W., Jr., Shearer, M. The child's call for help. *Mich. Med.,* July 1968, 67(13), 846–51.

Wahl, C. Suicide precipitated by psychotherapy: A clinical contribution. *Amer. J. Psychother.,* 1957, 25, 18–26.

Wallace, M.A. The nurse in suicide prevention. *Nurs. Outlook,* March 1967, 14(3), 55–7.

Wallerstein, R.S., Smelser, N. Psychoanalysis and sociology. *Internat. J. Psycho-Anal.,* 1968, 50, 693–710.

Warren, Max. On suicide. *Journal of the American Psychoanalytic Association,* 1976, 24(1), 199–234.

Weisman, A.D., Worden, J.W. Risk-rescue rating in suicide assessment. *Arch. Gen. Psychiatry,* June 1972, 26(6), 553–60.

Weitzel, W.D. Changing law and clinical dilemmas. *Am. J. Psychiatry,* March 1977, 134(3), 293–5.

West, D.J. *Murder followed by suicide.* Cambridge, Mass.: Harvard University Press, 1967.

Wetzel, R.D., McClure, J.N., Jr., Reich, T. Premenstrual symptoms in self-referrals to a suicide prevention service. *Br. J. Psychiatry,* Nov. 1971, 119 (552), 525–6.

Wetzel, R.D., Reich, T., McClure, J.N., Jr. Phase of the menstrual cycle and self-referrals to a suicide prevention service. *Br. J. Psychiatry,* Nov. 1971, 119 (552), 523–4.

Wilkins, J. Suicide calls and identification of suicidal callers. *Med. J. Aust.,* Oct. 21, 1972, 2(17), 923–9.

Wilkins, J.L. Experience in suicide prevention: Calls for help in Chicago. *Ill Med. J.,* March 1970, 137(3), 257–60 Passim.

Williams, A.H. Rape-murder. In R. Slovenko (Ed.), *Sexual behavior and the law.* Springfield, Ill.: C.C. Thomas, 1965.

Wolfgang, M.E. Suicide by means of the victim-precipitated homicide. In Resnik, H.L.P. (ed.): *Suicidal behaviors: Diagnosis and management.* Boston: Little, Brown, & Co, 1968.

Yufit, R.I., Loomis, S.D. The Suicide Assessment Team (SAT) in a general hospital. *Ill. Med. J.,* Dec. 1974, 146(6), 555–7.

Zee, H.J. Blindspots in recognizing serious suicidal intentions. *Bull Menninger Clin.,* Sept. 1972, 36(5), 551–5.

Zilborg, G. Suicide among civilized and primitive races. *Amer. J. Psychiat.,* 1936, 92, 1347–1396.

INDEX